KENNY
THE KOALA BEAR
IN THE LAND OF MEAN

By: A. J. J. Pierson

To: Joseph
May this book be
A blessing in your
walk with the King!
For His Glory †
A. J. J. Pierson

With thanksgiving to the King of Kings, for His Grace and Mercy given throughout my whole life;

And for Kim, who is an ever-present sign of the King's love for me.

Chapter One

Kenny always knew he was different. Brown as richest cocoa, his coloring was not like those of all the other koala bears. But, it never really bothered him. His sweet nature caused the other koalas to cease their teasing and actually be drawn to him. His eyes were black as coals yet with a warmth that was welcoming. Kenny really didn't have any enemies in Crystal Creek. And that is why it was such a shock to the gentle folk who lived there when Kenny went missing.

Greedy Gertie sat sprawl legged, counting her coins. If there was one thing that Greedy Gertie loved to do, it was to count how much money she had. She was undeniably the most selfish person on the planet. And, if you bothered to ask her, she would tell you that she was very proud of this fact. Yes, indeed, she had worked very, very hard to become the most selfish person in existence.

Not only did she like to count her own wealth, she liked to take that which belonged to others. And, she had absolutely no conscience. She never stayed awake at night wondering whom she might have hurt through her dirty, deceitful ways. Not Greedy Gertie. She was proud of this fact too. That she had long ago obliterated all trace of conscience and decency within her. Her soul was as black as soot. Not one glimmer of light could penetrate its greasy, grimy core.

Her breath was foul as well. And she smelled like rotting fish. The odor came from deep within her and it did not matter how many baths she took, because the inside of her remained ugly and dark and found its way out through her pores. She fashioned herself to be quite a beauty outwardly, although others often had a differing opinion on this regard. She had long black hair, which matched her crow-like demeanor. Her bangs stuck out this way and that way in razor-like spikes. She was not well educated, although she thought she was quite bright. When she got excited, she hopped about like a toad and her voice was as shrill as a banshee's. Her favorite phrase of all time was "it's all in black and white, it's all in black and white" which she would shriek out with vengeful vehemence when she was cheating others out of their belongings via a dirty contract written by her sly lawyers.

Oh, and, she absolutely relished the times of being angry! This was at least six times per day (on the low end). She loved to scream and throw tantrums and say ugly things to people. She did so to get her way. It so worked! Her husband, Pugnacious Pomposity, III, always gave in to her. He and his predecessors got their name due to always keeping their noses lifted high in the air. Pugnacious Pomposity, III particularly delighted in peering over his spectacles, which rested on the tip of his long nose, in the most condescending way to the rest of humanity, which was, in his conceited opinion, so far beneath him. He was a cowardly sort of fellow and felt it best to go along with whatever Greedy Gertie wanted in order to keep the peace of his home. After all, he had only married her to be his cook, maid, and to bear his two spoiled brat children, Horatio the Horrible and Salena the Shrieker. For Pugnacious Pomposity, III, all that mattered anyway were outward appearances and money, money, money and more money. Moreover, a not so bright, hot-tempered partner was fine because she fit the bill of tending to all of his selfish needs. Oh, what a wretched bunch of sorry snits this family was!

They lived in the Land of Mean. Along with other folk of like ilk. There were the Grab-A-Lots, quite a large clan whose hands were always where they should not be. Then there were the Smudge Pots, a very isolated group due to the filth that they wallowed in. In addition, were the Foot-In-Mouths, who spoke aloud every thought that popped into their fool brains like a rapid-fire pistol, destroying relationships with every ping, pop and zing.

It was quite a land, this Land of Mean. Nothing beautiful grew there. It was a stark, dry, dead landscape that only sported gnarled trees that were permanently grey, and sharp, spiny cacti that if brushed against, would dig their hooks into tender skin with a vengeance. There were no grass, flowers, creeks or streams. Just brown, dusty earth. Lots of rocks. And inhabitants who thought only about themselves.

Crystal Creek was surrounded by the most beautiful and verdant eucalyptus trees. The forty-foot giants made for quite the playground for an active bear like Kenny. He loved to frolic amongst these towering trees and listen to their leaves rustling gently in the breeze. He would frequently eat his fill of these tasty leaves 'til his belly bulged. Sometimes, he would feel the frisk of adventure stir within him, especially if it was a cool morning, and he would venture to the very border of this secure jungle-like divide and peer through it to the stark landscape that lay beyond Crystal Creek's lush world of rolling green hills, ponds, flower dotted meadows, lakes and streams. His mother said that evil people lived beyond their eucalyptus-lined borders and he was not to venture out of this safe world that was Kenny's home. Thieves and dangerous folk lurked about in that barren wasteland, she said. Not the place for such a tender, loving bear. But sometimes even the best of mothers can't know the mission of destiny their offspring are bound to fulfill.

Hannah was enjoying her quiet morning time with the King. Her fingers flew with fluidity over the piano keys in the sunlit study. Plants bedecked the room. The colors of greens, some with flowers, others just long and lush, gave life to the room. Hannah's cat, Puss Puss B' Guss Guss, (the "B" pronounced "Buh" and "Guss" rhyming with "Puss") a white, long-haired Ragdoll cat with gorgeous sky blue eyes, dreamed happily while curled in his kitty basket on a bench where the sunlight warmed his fur. Hannah's singing and playing songs to her King did not wake him from his slumber.

Hannah herself was a child of astonishing beauty. Her long blonde hair glistened like spun gold in the sunlight and her green eyes shone with a depth that belied her 11 years of age. The beauty within her soul was what truly made her a shining star though among the Crystal Creek folk. Her generosity knew no measure complimenting her kind and gentle spirit. Yet, there was an inner strength behind that gentleness that attracted others to her. She did not have a selfish bone in her body and mean spiritedness was something quite foreign to her.

Her parents, Judith and Daniel Stillwaters, had instilled such qualities in their young one from babyhood. Mrs. Stillwaters was always doing some act of kindness to a neighbor, from helping tend to a sick child to taking food to those who were struggling and in need. Mr. Stillwaters was on many charitable boards in the community and gave away a good portion of his income to help those who were found wanting. He saw money as a tool to help others, not as something to covet and grasp and worship as a god. This was a happy, peaceful home--a home in order--a home with purpose--a home where love flowed from the King of Kings into the hearts of those who dwelled therein.

Hannah paused in her piano worship and skipped into the kitchen. She felt a leading in her spirit to make some cookies to take down the street where the Pomposity children lived. Even though they never treated her very nicely when she went to visit them, she was determined to continue her acts of kindness with the hopes that one day they might know the light and love that she felt in her heart.

"Momma, would it be all right with you if I made some chocolate chip cookies to take over to Horatio the Horrible and Salena the Shrieker's house after lunch?" asked Hannah. The Stillwaters' home was a modest older house on the edge of Crystal Creek. The folks on their block didn't have lots of money, but made up for it in love and warm hearts. Their home was only about four blocks from the beginning of the Land of Mean. The Pomposities' house was another six blocks from that point located in the midst of the wealthy section of the influential elite of the Land of Mean.

Mrs. Stillwaters was herself busy making up a care basket filled with home baked goodies for a new mother in their neighborhood. Judith Stillwaters was at her finest in the kitchen: baking bread, bustling about as she concocted mouth-watering recipes for her family. Hannah loved to watch her mother there, as it seemed as if there was a special glow about her when she was cooking. Poetry in motion, as her father often lovingly exclaimed.

"Yes, dear, that would be fine. However, please remember: when you go there with the gift of the cookies, don't let your heart get discouraged if their words and actions are unkind. You are a sensitive one and I hate to see you hurt."

"I won't, momma--promise!" *Not like the last time,* she thought, when she had come home in tears because Horatio had ripped the arm off her favorite doll that she was showing to his sister, Salena. Momma was able to fix it though on her trusty sewing machine.

"You know, sometimes it takes longer to break through folks' hard exteriors--sort of like different types of nuts. Take the almond, for example, pretty easily cracked--unlike the Brazil nut or..."

Momma was on a roll, mused Hannah. She could fixate on a topic for hours--but, it was always pretty interesting and it was just due to the intense and deep nature momma possessed. She listened to momma's oral dissertation on the hardness and softness of nuts while busying herself with her cookie batter. Soon the delicious aroma of

9

chocolate chip cookies baking wafted throughout the house and Hannah eagerly awaited that first bite into gooey chocolate goodness.

Puss Puss B' Guss Guss surveyed the landscape from on high atop his kitty tree. Fall had come with the beautiful paintbrush display of golds, reds and yellow greens. Winter was soon to come on its heels with its icy winds and fields filled with frigid snow. Puss Puss shivered remembering Hannah's delight in dipping his paws in winter's first snow while cheerfully exclaiming: "See, Puss Puss--it's cold, isn't it?" *Every year the same silly ritual. You would think she would remember that we cats are smart--not like those drooly, slobbery canines that have brains the size of peas. We actually remember things! And, we keep ourselves clean,* he mused as he began again another round of incessant ritual bathing that was his nature to do. *After all, I am a white cat, not grey, not black, but white, and this fur takes much effort,* he fussed. Puss Puss B' Guss Guss was intently chewing on a difficult hind paw nail when Hannah flounced in the room and ruffled all of his newly cleaned fur. *Honestly, how is one to stay clean when my fur is constantly being messed with and...oh sigh, it feels soo good though.* Puss Puss' complaining gave place to deep rumbling purrs of satisfaction as Hannah's fingers skritched all of his favorite spots. He rolled over exposing his bountiful fluffy belly, which was Hannah's cue to rub and scratch. As Puss Puss' purrs grew louder with eyes closed and head stretched back, Hannah gently rubbed his chin. *Oh, this is what heaven must be like,* purred Puss Puss B' Guss Guss forgetting his former agitation over having his fur disheveled.

"You are such a sweet kitsa kitty," intoned Hannah. "My special baby. Momma loves you!" Puss Puss B' Guss Guss' blue eyes opened briefly to gaze at his mommy Hannah with an expression of pure kitty bliss.

"Well, I'm off to the Pomposities', Puss Puss--see you in a bit." Puss Puss was so relaxed now that he couldn't move if he had wanted to. And he didn't. *Catnap number five for the day coming on,* he thought sleepily as Hannah left the room and bounced out the front door and down the steps.

Chapter Two

The Pomposity home was in an uproar. Which was not unusual. Pugnacious Pomposity, III had just left for work leaving Greedy Gertie to the distasteful task of tending to their ill tempered and terribly spoiled twosome, Horatio the Horrible, and Salena the Shrieker. The Pomposity children were appropriately named as Horatio's actions were nothing but horrible, and Salena had the obnoxious and frequent habit of wailing at the top of her lungs whenever she did not get her way. These were long episodes that even caused Horatio to put his hands over his ears while Pugnacious and Gertie pretended not to hear because their children were picture perfect and could never do anything wrong.

As soon as Pugnacious Pomposity, III's car was out of the driveway and heading down the street for work of a morning, Greedy Gertie would cease her waving to him out the living room window and leap off the couch, in her characteristic toad-like demeanor, and whisk to her bedroom. She would then securely lock her door leaving her renegade children to fend for themselves for the next couple of hours. Sometimes she would run a bubble bath where she would soak for at least an hour and turn up the radio to her favorite station loud enough to drown out the screams, bangs and thumps of unhappy children in the next room. At other times, she would get on the phone with her best friend, Slanderous Suzie of the Foot-In-Mouth-Clan, and they would gossip for hours, destroying their so-called other friends with their vicious tongues.

This a.m. Horatio was on a particularly horrible streak as he snuck up behind Salena who was playing with her favorite doll, and he yanked her hair so hard that he left her screaming shrilly with several strands pulled out and now stuck to his jelly sticky hands. He then kicked over the play table where Salena had just moments before set up her tea set for a tea party for herself and her dolls. She had actually put real tea (cold of course) into the little pot and now its contents flew in a spray onto the white living room carpet creating a pattern of brown blotches and streams. The little cups and saucers didn't make it to the carpet like the teapot did, but instead, shattered into tiny fragments on the hard kitchen floor. Of course, Salena, though only six years old, was not given cheap plastic tea sets like the other children her age. No, no. Her mother and father only bought the best and most expensive for their precious. Oh, well. Another $200.00 china tea set down the drain.

The same was true for the earrings Salena wore in her pierced ears. Only real diamonds and rubies would do. None of those simulated gemstones that the poor unfortunate children had to wear. And these always were lost--at least a pair a week. But these children were trained that it didn't matter. Their mom and dad would replace it. No care needed to be taken with their things. Spending money and flaunting their possessions, even their children's possessions, gave the Pomposities a thrill of power and importance. Truly intoxicating.

As Hannah came down the street, she could hear Salena's screams. Which really didn't surprise her. The home she was about to visit was always in a state of chaos and turmoil. Particularly when Mr. Pomposity was at work. Hannah said a quick prayer in her heart to the King of Kings to give her strength as she reached for the doorbell. The cookies were still somewhat warm and she relished the smell emanating from the little basket she had carefully wrapped and tucked them into. She took a deep breath and fortified herself for what lay behind the door.

Hannah didn't have to wait long. She heard the sound of running feet that slammed into the door before it was flung open. It was Horatio, smears of jelly from breakfast still clinging to the edges of his 9-year-old mouth and chin. Still in pajamas that were designer silk with a monogrammed "H" on the pocket, he glared at Hannah wondering what she could possibly want and was about to tell her to get lost when he spied the basket in her hands and saw the very tip of a cookie peeking its way out the top. Without even a greeting, he reached out and yanked the basket from her hands and took off running back down the hallway of the Pomposity home to his room. Hannah's cry of "wait a minute" as she stepped over the threshold of their house, was answered by the resounding slam of Horatio's bedroom door. Sighing, Hannah ventured further into the Pomposities' living room to where Salena now sat cross-legged in front of the brocade couch where the teapot had found a resting place, wailing hysterically at decibels loud enough to cause any dog within earshot to send up its own baleful moaning.

As Hannah gazed at the tear-drenched wailer, she felt a sense of compassion and concern unusual for her 11 tender years. Hannah had the unique ability to see beyond the obvious and to look deeper beneath the surface appearances, a trait she most probably had developed from the like-minded spirit of her mother. Looking at Salena, she didn't just see a spoiled little girl who most assuredly had too much expensive "stuff" to know what to do with. Instead, she saw a hurting child that longed for things that money just could not ever buy. No amount of expensive toys, dresses or jewelry could fill the holes in the heart of this child that these wails ultimately came from. Hannah knew that this wailing could one day be replaced by beautiful songs when this heart came to know who and what Hannah had already discovered. But this knowing would take patience and time.

Hannah's reflections were abruptly interrupted by the harsh grating cry of "What is going on out here?!" as Greedy Gertie, the Pomposity children's mother, came into the room like a blast of cold winter air--chilling to the very bone. As Greedy Gertie surveyed the disaster of fragmented tea set dishes in the kitchen and the ugly brown splotches that were now a permanent feature of the once white living room carpet that the Pomposity children were forbidden to play upon, fear gripped Salena's heart. She stopped her ear splitting wailing to sputter out with her finger outstretched and pointed towards Hannah: "She did it."

Greedy Gertie, who had been fully ready to let her anger loose upon her children, now turned with a vehemence towards Hannah who, astonished at Salena's accusations, had risen up away from her.

"You little do gooder, always coming over to this home uninvited." The hatred in her tone and the wicked look in Greedy Gertie's eyes caused Hannah to now step backwards out of the living room making her way as quickly as she could to the entryway and the possibility of escape.

"Don't you know that you are not welcome here," Gertie bellowed onward, "You are not of our class of people. You don't know the value of expensive homes and toys. Take your rag-a-muffin self and get out of our house!"

As Hannah walked backward across the living room, Greedy Gertie followed, face twisted in a grimace, arms flailing in angled gestures, and her long, black crow colored hair swinging in rhythm, continuing her tirade. "I would ask your mother and father to pay for this damage, but they are too poor to afford the things we love. Just get out of here and don't ever come back!"

Her last epithet ended on such a high shrill note that Horatio opened his bedroom door a crack to peer through out of curiosity just in time to see Hannah run through the entryway and out the living room door. Chuckling to himself, he quietly closed and locked his door behind him. Wiping the leftover crumbs of Hannah's delicious cookies from his mouth, Horatio the Horrible gave a swift kick to the now empty basket sending it flying under his bed.

Hannah flew up the front steps to her home, two at a time. She flung the front door open, letting it bang shut behind her as she raced to her room. This door she closed with vigor as well (slamming actually) to give an exclamation point to the feelings raging within her. She was no longer scared or sad--she was angry! Furious, in fact. *How dare that Pomposity woman talk to me like that?! I didn't do anything wrong--I was just trying to do something nice for her kids and then I get blamed for their messes--fine! If she doesn't want me over there, I just won't go--who wants to play with a couple of brats anyway?* Hannah's thoughts raged through her mind in quite a rambling fashion whenever she got mad. She paced about her room as she thought, tossing a pillow here and there for emphasis. *I will never do anything nice for them again--not ever!* And with that, she threw herself on her bed to ponder what a wasted morning this had been.

A soft knock interrupted her chaotic thoughts. "Hannah, can I come in?" momma's gentle voice queried. Hannah simply could not bring herself to respond. "Hannah, please. I think we need to talk."

At this moment, talking was not what Hannah wanted. She would really like to hit someone. Hard. And repeatedly. Maybe Horatio for grabbing all the cookies for himself that she had put so much effort and time into making. *Yes, that would make me feel better.*

The door opened and momma was looking at her with the compassion and wisdom in her eyes that only comes from years of experience, trials and time spent with the Master. Looking at eyes like those with the thoughts she had just been thinking caused Hannah to turn her gaze downward and to stare at the multi-colored, quilted bed cover.

"I gather that things did not go well for you over at the Pomposity house," momma said softly as she sat down on the bed beside Hannah's sprawled body. "Can we talk about it? I know you will feel better once you let it out," she said stroking Hannah's hair. The soft touch caused Hannah's anger to melt away and now tears began to flow freely down her cheeks.

"Oh, momma--it was awful--just awful!" And between sobs, the whole torrid story emerged. Hannah and momma hugged throughout and several tissues lay crumpled on the bed after it was over. Momma listened until all the emotion was gone and Hannah was calm. Then momma's wisdom came through in gentle, yet firm tones.

"You know, Hannah, what you were dealing with here is not just spoiled children or a mean-tempered parent. No, honey, it is much deeper than that. You were dealing with spiritual blindness--dark v. light, truth v. lies. When you went to their home, you went in the light, strength and generosity of the King. What you were met with were the puny spirits of selfishness, meanness and lack of self-control. Chaos was already raging in their home before you got there--once you did, a real battle began. You brought the light that emanates from our majestic King into a home where darkness rules."

"But, momma," interrupted Hannah, "isn't light stronger than darkness?" Why didn't the light win? Did I do something wrong?"

"No, my dear. You did nothing wrong. You are still growing in spiritual things and were just a bit overwhelmed. Greedy Gertie can be quite a sight when she is on a rampage and fear grabbed hold of you. Fear stops our minds from working right if we give in to it. It can become a near paralyzing force actually. But, the spirit of light and truth is far greater than fear. Once you can truly grasp that fact, you'll see more success in these types of encounters."

"But, not to fret," momma soothed standing up and straightening her smock. "Let's take a break from all of this and go out in the garden for a bit of fresh air. I have some tulips that must get in the ground before our first frost. Digging in the dirt is good for the soul."

Chapter Three

Rick the Red-Necked Ranger loved his job. Deep in the Pine Valley forest near Crystal Creek stood his watch tower from which he could not only spy out every area of the deep verdant valley beneath him, but with his special military-style binoculars, Rick could also see many of the meadows bordering his forest. He took great pride in his job--being a Johnny on the spot for a wide variety of tasks. Early in the day, he would climb this lofty tower with his thermos of piping hot coffee strapped in a pack on his back, tool belt jangling against the metal as he ascended in the crisp morning air. To Rick, this was not just a job. It was a vocation of the soul. The quiet of the rustling pines soothed his inner being. Not that this was a totally cushy job, however. It required him to be alert for potential dangers, such as the dreaded forest fires and to sound the alert with lightning speed. Sometimes he had to organize reconnaissance missions to rescue a child who had wandered away from a family campsite. At other times, it was his keen engineering and fix-it skills that were called upon in the many ranger stations located throughout the park.

Rick was a happy fellow for the most part. His ability to find humor in most everything brought joy and eased folks' minds when tensions ran high. But he could turn from his joking demeanor to one serious, not to be dismissed, hard-line kind of a guy if there was danger about. And that gift was soon to be tested and put a demand upon which even for Rick, would be a battle never seen before in these parts.

Gertie was still fuming. "That little brat Hannah," she crowed to no one in particular. Salena had escaped to her own room after Hannah had fled their home and Horatio had fallen asleep in his room after his cookie gorging fest. It was best to stay out of Greedy Gertie's way when she was in a state; the children had learned this the hard way and many sore bottoms later.

"Look at this mess. I just can't deal with it a moment more." And with that declaration, Gertie went outside. Toys were strewn about the backyard. The pea gravel was scattered about with bare dirt showing through from the children's play. The immense pool could have used a cleaning due to dirt kicked to its bottom by Horatio the Horrible, but Greedy Gertie did not give it a second glance as she slipped out the back gate. She felt a need to wander. Somewhere. Anywhere. She didn't feel like packing the children into the van for a trip to the mall. No. Not in a mood to deal with them in an enclosed space today after all that uproar. She wanted something different. An adventure. *Apart from these brats of mine. And all of their incessant demands. They won't know I'm gone. Just a bit of a stroll. Clear my head. Then perhaps I'll feel like taking them some-where. And buying myself some new jewelry!*

Greedy Gertie kept on in her ugly ramblings. Behind her home lay a ravine which let out, if followed, into a desert area beyond the suburbia she so relished living in. She rarely came out this way, but today she felt a need to just get away from everyone, especially those noisy, pesky kids.

Kenny the Koala Bear had spotted a butterfly flitting about amongst the lush eucalyptus leaves. He absolutely loved butterflies and this one was so incredibly gorgeous! Its blues and magentas glistened in the sunlight as it playfully flitted just above Kenny's grasp. Sometimes it would pause and Kenny would draw closer for a better look. Just as he would get within paws reach, it would take off again up and down, in and out of the towering majestic trees. Kenny the Koala Bear leaped and bounced his way after it in playful abandon. So intent was he in his game of hide and seek the butterfly that he didn't notice that he had leapt beyond the borders of Crystal Creek and into the sparse wasteland that was the Land of Mean.

Greedy Gertie squinted her beady eyes. Far in the distance, beyond that saguaro cactus, something was hopping. A funny looking brown thing. *Like a rolling brown ball,* thought Gertie. *What on earth could that be?,* she wondered. She had never seen anything moving in such a fashion. It seemed to bound and leap and then sort of bounce and roll. Nothing she had ever seen or knew of could do that.

I must get closer. But, careful. Could be dangerous. A little thrill went through Greedy Gertie at the thought. *Can't let it spy me first, though.* She began stealthily creeping along, hiding herself behind rock formations in the dry, dusty gully. Just cacti and rocks. She was careful to not brush against the extra spiny ones as, if they grabbed a hold of you, you were in for some serious pain. Bit by bit she drew closer and then peered cautiously around some particularly large rocks that she crouched behind. As she snuck a peek, what she saw made her gasp. *Why, it was a little brown colored bear! Batting and bouncing and rolling--why, it looked like a toy come to life!* Gertie rubbed her eyes and squinted against the sun. Gertie was actually quite near sighted--a fact that pride would not allow her to admit to anyone. She didn't want to wear glasses for she feared her beauty would be compromised and contact lenses were not an option as the idea of actually sticking something in her eyes turned her stomach in queasiness.

Was this a real bear? But, it was so small, how could this be possible? Was it a trick? Maybe a remote control, battery operated bear. Wow, won't my kids be the talk and envy of the neighborhood if I can capture it and take it home to them! But, with what?

Greedy Gertie started looking about for something, anything with which she could contain this bear. She spied something black and flapping from under a rock up ahead. Treading quietly (just in case this was a real animal and not a toy) she inched forward and saw that what was flapping was an old, large, plastic trash bag. Besides being a bit oily from who knows what, it would suffice for the job at hand.

Grasping the bag in one hand, Greedy Gertie stealthily inched forward. She was now about 20 feet from the bear, now 15, now 10, and then......*whoosh!* She threw the bag over Kenny the Koala Bear, whose back had been to her the whole time in his intense escapade with the butterfly. And then, with another quick maneuver, Gertie flipped the bag upward and tied it shut. Kenny was plunged into abject darkness with the stench of old frying oil combined with the suffocating odor of dead fish making it quite unpleasant as well as difficult to breathe. He gasped out a terrified "Help" and then "Please let me out--I can't breathe" before he became quiet as there just wasn't enough air to continue a struggle. And, he was being banged about onto something hard that was quite unpleasant. *Oh, my,* thought Kenny the Koala Bear, *what has happened here?* Silently, with tears tumbling onto his now oily chocolate fur, he communed with his King.

Greedy Gertie was picking up the pace now with her ill-gotten gain flung over her shoulder. Her steps were a cross between a toad-like hop (which she tended to do when excited or angry) and a run. This caused the sack, containing poor Kenny, to come down every other step with quite a thump onto Gertie's bony back. It didn't bother Greedy Gertie in the least as she was not only insensitive emotionally, but physically as well, and her back had little feeling to it. But, for poor Kenny, each *thwump* and *bump* against Gertie's back was quite painful, and disturbingly jarring in spite of his furry padding for Kenny the Koala Bear was both tenderhearted inside as well as sensitive on the outside. And the plastic bag didn't muffle Greedy Gertie's shrill shrieks, which hurt his ears as well.

"Ooh, wait 'til they see...wait 'til they see...a bear, fluffy and fine and all for me!" Greedy Gertie wasn't much of a poet, but she was tickled that she had made this rhyme, however short and crudely formed, and she kept shrieking it as she hopped towards home.

Katie Koala, Kenny the Koala Bear's mother, had been expecting Kenny to come in any moment now for his daily afternoon snack of honey sesame crunch cookies with an emphasis on the <u>honey</u>. In fact, Katie was surprised that he hadn't come in by now as the smell of the cookies baking and filtering through the screen door down to Kenny's favorite eucalyptus tree grove was usually enough to bring that always ravenous bear in for a snack.

Katie looked at the clock in her kitchen. *My, how time had flown today!* It was already 3:30. She had been so busy with laundry and cleaning (as was her weekly Friday ritual) that she had scarcely had time to admonish Kenny to not venture beyond their borders. He was such a joy, although a bit too curious at times, but really, no major troubles with Kenny. So good-natured, playful and tenderhearted. Quick to say he was sorry if he hurt someone's feelings or tracked in mud for the umpteenth time on a freshly mopped floor. No, he was definitely a bear without guile--never with an intent to do any wrong to anyone. *Now, where is this bear of mine? The cookies will be cold soon if he doesn't scamper through that door in the next few minutes. And, he so likes them warm. Better go and check on him and see what he's gotten himself into,* thought Katie.

Greedy Gertie could hardly contain herself. "What a find, what a find!" she exclaimed aloud. Banging through the back gate, Kenny the Koala Bear got quite a whack as the gate hit him squarely between the shoulders before slamming shut. He winced in pain, but not a squeal came out as the foul, stuffy air in the wretched plastic bag was truly doing him in. Gertie hopped through the yard almost tripping on Salena's tricycle in the process. Cursing, she slid open the back sliding door and bellowed: "Children, where are you? I've got something amazing to show you!"

Nothing had been cleaned up since the early afternoon fiasco. Shattered tea set pieces were strewn about the kitchen floor. The living room still sported the ugly, now nearly dry, brown tea stains on the rug. And Salena's teapot still maintained its new home forlornly in front of the expensive brocade couch that only company and adults were allowed to rest their posteriors upon.

The children were nowhere in sight. Cursing again, Greedy Gertie increased the volume of her shrill cry and changed it into a demand: "Get out here now or else!"

The shrillness broke through Horatio the Horrible's slumber and jarred him bolt awake. His full belly from the cookies he had gorged himself with earlier had caused him to fall asleep in the middle of his video game. The controller slid off his lap as he started upright on his bed and continued onto the floor with a dull thud. The game was still on his television set, its red and yellow flashes from exploding, make-believe bombs reflected off of the light blue walls of his room. Almost had made it to the third level of "Kill Them or Die", the hottest game on the market. He remembered the fit he had pitched to get it. His dad stood in the dark, cold, early morning air outside the video store to buy this limited edition set the first day it went on sale. But his mom's incessant screaming is what concerned him now as he knew if he didn't respond quickly there would be a sore rear end from her belt thwacks.

Coming down the hallway, he saw that his little brat sister, Salena the Shrieker, was already out in the playroom adjacent to the kitchen with his mom. He hated her so much. She got way too much attention from his parents and they were always fawning over her, telling her how pretty she was and praising her when she was dressed up in that stupid ballerina outfit prancing about the house like some kind of cotton candy fairy. Yuk!

But, hey, what was mom holding and droning on about? Maybe it's a present for me! He broke into a run and slid on the floor in his stocking feet right into Salena pushing her off balance and she fell with a bang to the floor on her knees. She began wailing which drowned out what his mom had been saying.

"Horatio, you clumsy child--you've hurt your sister!" Greedy Gertie set the black sack down that she had been holding a moment before to scoop up Salena the Shrieker in order to comfort her. Seeing the bag unattended was all that Horatio the Horrible needed. He lunged forward, grabbed the bag, and took off with it into the forbidden-to-children living room. He only had a few precious seconds before they would catch up with him. Hastily, he tore open the black plastic bag. The stench of oil and rotted fish greeted him with a pungent sting to his nostrils. He couldn't see a thing in there with his head stuck in the bag and that odor made him flinch backwards. *Fine, I'll just dump out whatever it is* and with that resolve, he yanked the bag upward and over and Kenny the Koala Bear fell with an oily *thwump* onto the white carpet of the Pomposity living room floor.

"Kenny, Kenny, where are you? Cookies are ready and warm," Katie Koala hollered as she raised a paw to block out the sun's glare as she looked down the well-worn path to the eucalyptus tree grove. No answer came to her straining ears. Only the pretty tones of a cardinal singing in the large oak next to the pond on the side of their home. Another favorite play spot for Kenny. *Where has that bear got off to? It's just not like him to not be near at this time of day.* Katie was now almost all the way down the grassy path to the point where it rose up to a knoll where one could see downward onto the lush eucalyptus grove. No sign of Kenny. Momma Katie hollered again-- just in case he was off to the sides out of view. "Kenny, Kenny, where are you--cookies are warm and waiting." But no response answered her pleas. *This is so strange,* she thought heading back down the path and turning past the house out towards the pond.

It was a gorgeous view with the sun glistening off the placid pond's green and blue hues. Seagulls could be seen in a white flock on its farthest shore, so many in number that it looked like they were having a convention of sorts to discuss important issues of bird relevance as they flocked and skittered about among the pebbles. Weeping willows hung their long, flowing, wispy, drooping branches on this side of the pond, a place Kenny the Koala Bear also loved to hide beneath when they were in full leaf in the heat of summer. A family of turtles lay in symmetrical formation sunning themselves on a fallen log that extended out into the pond's watery depths of beauty. And, over there, next to the towering oak that stood inland from the pond, was the family picnic table where many a happy summer meal was enjoyed in shaded bliss on hot summer days. But amidst all this placid beauty, no sign of Kenny. Momma Katie fought off pangs of worry beginning to grip her mind with the thought that perhaps he had wandered over to their good friend's house, the Sunflowers. She went inside to give Winnie Sunflower a call.

Chapter Four

By now, Salena's screams had quieted down due to Greedy Gertie's coddling. Though she was a mean-spirited mother, Greedy Gertie loved to dote on her daughter as she saw her as a reflection of herself--a mirror image, so to speak--a "Greedy Gertie" in training. Greedy Gertie loved to lavish expensive dresses, jewelry and presents on her young daughter as her desire was to train her to be as selfish and vain as she was and to only value that which glistened, glittered or was made of gold. She wanted her daughter to realize that only money mattered and people were always expendable. Frequent ventures to the exclusive shops in the mall were part of the training to this end as were the episodes of ignoring other people's feelings and thinking only of what would benefit oneself as Greedy Gertie was the ever ready and daily example of. Her unabashed and unashamed favoritism of Salena the Shrieker over Horatio the Horrible was her course of emotional cruelty 101 for her little princess to perpetuate in the future.

Salena the Shrieker, carried by her mother, had now made it to where Horatio the Horrible crouched over Kenny the Koala Bear in the oily puddle that was rapidly soaking into the lush carpet. "Ooh, Horatio, you have the brain the size of a flea," screamed Greedy Gertie so loudly next to Horatio's ear that he flinched backward in a start. As he had been so intently focused on the bear, he had not heard Mother Gertie creeping up behind him. "Now you've got that horrid oil all in the carpet!" she ranted. "This bear was my surprise--why couldn't you wait and let me open the bag?!" Gertie was now shaking Horatio by the shoulders with a vengeance as she had set Salena down. Salena now had the opportunity to peer between her mother's legs at the strange looking, oily, smelly brown bear lying motionless on the once pristine living room floor. She ventured around her mother who was still so caught up in her screaming tirade that she was oblivious to all else--for the moment, anyway. Salena the Shrieker got down on her knees and crawled closer to see what this thing was that Greedy Gertie thought was so great.

The bear looked like it was soft but she was afraid to touch it because of the rancid, oily smell inflaming her nostrils as she drew nearer peering down at the bear. His eyes looked almost real--shiny black, but not like the toy bears at the store. These seemed to draw her in as if she was looking into a deep pond of water where you could see shapes beneath the surface. There was something so real here. Almost like this bear was alive!

Greedy Gertie finally stopped shaking Horatio the Horrible and turned to see Salena the Shrieker on all fours over Kenny the Koala Bear. "Move away, Salena," she demanded. And grabbing Kenny with her bony fingers by his leg, she pulled him from underneath Salena's crouched position and propped him up next to the coffee table. "He moves and jumps and bounces. I thought when I first saw him that he was a real bear, but, he's obviously just some kind of electronic toy. Give him a moment. I bet he will start up again."

What a strange sight this would have been to anyone walking in upon this scene. Two young children, one still with muffled sobs from his shaking and one adult all sitting cross-legged while staring at an oily, smelly, dark brown koala bear propped up next to a coffee table waiting for it to move. The grandfather clock in the entry hall echoed loudly with its tick tocking away the seconds in the heavy with anticipation silence as the trio stared. The koala bear remained stationary.

What broke this strange silence was the sound of the side garage door opening. "Daddy's home!" squealed Salena the Shrieker and she went racing down the side hallway to be swept up in his arms. "How's my sweet little princess?" cooed Pugnacious Pomposity, III. Horatio the Horrible also abandoned Greedy Gertie to greet his father. "And how is my soon to be Nobel Prize winner?" Pugnacious Pomposity, III thought his son to be the smartest child around and would tell anyone who would listen to a painfully boring as well as irritating tale about how Horatio could read full-length chapter books when he had just turned three years of age. (In actuality, Horatio the Horrible could only sound out the words at that tender age with absolutely no clue as to the actual meaning of the words, but Mr. Pomposity could not be told this fact by anyone as he was himself superior to everyone else's inferior simple-minded knowledge, in his opinion). After all, he <u>was</u> a Snob Yard graduate with a Ph.D. His dissertation thesis had been on the life cycle of the needle nosed, pin striped aboriginal beetle who burrowed thin snake like tunnels in the rotting tree trunk carcasses that littered the deep, dark, outback jungle land of Australia. He had been published in several issues of the infamous scientific magazine, *Snobs Who Know Too Much About One Subject*, printed annually by the Scientific Elite Society for North America.

As Mr. Arrogant *in persona,* (alias Pugnacious Pomposity, III) rounded the corner, he came face to face with the frightful disarray that the playroom and living room now sported replete with the odd view of his wife sitting on the floor looking with anticipation at some two-foot-tall, brown thing leaning against his late mother Abigail's antique mahogany marble-topped coffee table. And there was the most distasteful odor filling the room.

"Gertie, what on earth are you doing?" queried Pugnacious Pomposity, III in well-ordered tones. He prided himself at always being in control and sounding like the stuffed-shirt person that he so proudly was. Emotions were something that only the weak or the less intelligent displayed. And, one wildly emotional person per household was quite enough. Since he had not married Greedy Gertie for her intelligence, he could withstand her temper fits as well as her decidedly irrational behavior on occasions too numerous to tally.

"He's going to move--any moment now, he's going to move!" muttered Gertie, more to herself than to her husband, who had an incredulous look spreading across his unattractive features.

"What's going to move?"

"The bear, of course, nitwit." Greedy Gertie was the only one who could get away with derogatory names thrown Pugnacious Pomposity, III's way.

"Do you have a remote control of some sort?"

"No, he doesn't need one. He moves on his own."

"That's impossible, Gertie. He has to have some internal or external mechanism--perhaps an on/off switch." With this latest bit of intellectual wit displayed, Pugnacious set Salena down and reached beneath the coffee table and picked up Kenny the Koala Bear. He turned him this way and that looking for a switch, button, wire, anything. Without realizing it, in his zeal to show off his scientific, rational manner of approaching the situation, his turning of the bear had caused drips of the foul oil to spray upon his $800 Aristocati Pierre suit trousers.

"Daddy, daddy, you're getting oil on you," exclaimed Salena.

"Oh, my word." As he glanced downwards in horror at the splatters on his pants, he abruptly let go of Kenny the Koala Bear who fell first on his head and then rolled to his back.

"Oh, this is terrible--how distasteful--I must get these to the cleaners at once." And with that, Pugnacious Pomposity, III hightailed it out of the room.

Horatio ran after his dad and could be heard imploring him to take him with and "Can we get a pizza to bring home?" echoing out to the living room.

Greedy Gertie, hands stuck on her hips, was horribly disappointed and crestfallen due to the bear's lack of performance. She stared down at the motionless bear in great disgust.

"He probably got broken with all this banging about," she fumed. "And he stinks because of that stupid sack." *No matter. He's still mine,* she reassured herself. *I'll fix him up. Give him a good cleaning. He'll look good and I can display him when I want to.*

And with that resolve, Greedy Gertie scooped Kenny the Koala Bear up and headed to the kitchen sink to make up some suds to clean this, her strange possession.

It was starting to get dark. The pinks and reds of sunset were fading now. Katie Koala was pacing about the kitchen. Her calls to the neighbors and to any possible friends that Kenny could have wandered off to had been in vain. No one had seen Kenny. After several more trips to all of Kenny's favorite outdoor haunts, turning up neither hide nor hair of her precious koala son, Katie's frenzied searching had given way to deep-seated panic. *Something is terribly, terribly wrong--I have to get help. But, was it really time to call the headquarters? I'll give it two more hours--that's the most--then I will,* she resolved. *In the meantime, I'll pray.* And with that, she knelt beside the well-worn, wooden kitchen table and sent her mother's heart-rending pleas on high.

Greedy Gertie rubbed and scrubbed Kenny the Koala Bear's fur with the soap bubbles she scooped out of the kitchen sink makeshift cleaning station for project bear clean up. She didn't want to soak him because Gertie was still convinced that there was some type of electronic part in this bear that would come back to life. She would show everyone that she was right--that this bear could hop and bounce and do all sorts of tricks like she had seen him do with her own eyes out in the desert.

The scented foamy bubbles were doing the trick without getting the bear too wet. And the smell was fading away too. Greedy Gertie scrubbed with a fervor until every last oily place was clean. The children had left with Pugnacious Pomposity, III to take his suit trousers to the dry cleaners and then onward to Little Italy's Famous Pizza Pies to pick up a large sausage with the works pizza for dinner. Gertie rarely cooked even though she had the time. She much preferred to go out to eat or spend her husband's money on take out. Today provided an easy excuse as to why dinner wasn't ready. Sometimes, though, she had to stretch the truth (lie actually) in order to get taken out to dinner. She kept a list of excuses hidden in her sock drawer and checked them off and rotated them so that she wouldn't use the same one twice in a week. Her system worked so well on absent-minded Mr. Intellect (Pugnacious) that she usually only had to make a meal about once a week. And cold cereal worked for the children in the morning with lunch usually being at the mall.

Now that the bear was thoroughly scrubbed, Greedy Gertie took him to the master bedroom vanity to give him a good blow dry. The hair dryer's shrill whirring motor pierced the silence as Gertie reached down and grabbed a soft doll brush that Salena had dropped on the bedroom floor and she went to town with her fluff and dry. Soon, Kenny the Koala Bear looked quite amazingly transformed and Greedy Gertie held him at arm's length to admire her hard work. His chocolate brown fur actually glistened beneath the vanity mirror lights and felt as soft as a mink stole. His black shiny eyes and shiny nose really were quite life like. *My treasure,* thought Gertie.

Hmmm. I don't want those children's sticky pizza hands messing up my hard work after dinner. Where can I put him? As Greedy Gertie was looking about and contemplating this very matter, she heard Pugnacious' car pulling in the driveway and the electric whir of the garage door being automatically opened.

Quick, I must hide him. Suddenly the perfect place came to her devious mind. She went to the small middle drawer of her bureau where she kept a variety of small miscellaneous items--keys, separated earrings, broken jewelry--*oh, where is it?* She rummaged through the baubles, beads and trinkets to....*yes, there it is!* A very uniquely shaped, old-fashioned key to her late mother's cedar chest that was now housed in their attic. Grabbing the key in her greedy palm, she raced to the hallway and pushed the button that automatically lowered the stairs to the upper room. Kenny the Koala Bear was now tightly pressed to her chest as she frantically climbed the attic stairs.

The light switch was to her right as she fumbled for it on the wall after pulling herself into that dark, musty smelling place. As she flipped on the switch, she could see the old cedar chest way back at the far end of the attic under the window framed by faded blue lace curtains. Various boxes of all shapes, colors and sizes as well as numerous trunks littered the space and a thick coat of dust blanketed it all.

Hurry, hurry, she exhorted herself as she could now hear the van car doors being slammed below. The cedar chest was quite old, but still in good shape. One could actually sit on the top of it as it had a cushioned black leather seat. Quite a bit of carved work had been done on the fronts and sides and it would have been quite a lovely piece if it was oiled, dusted and cared for. Greedy Gertie hurriedly put the key in the dusty brass keyhole and with a loud click, it opened. The strong scent of mothballs greeted her like an old friend--Gertie loved this smell. Inside, were many treasures that Gertie would have to re-visit on another occasion. In haste, she put Kenny the Koala Bear on top of her late mother's hand-stitched wedding ring pattern quilt and with a loud slam and click of the lock, Kenny was enveloped by darkness once again. Greedy Gertie quickly thrust the key deep into her apron pocket and took off in her hopping run, managing to click off the attic light and barrel down the attic stairs. She rapidly punched the button to draw them upwards behind her, with her feet barely hitting the floor in the hallway just as the children and Pugnacious came banging in through the door to the garage, pizza box held high over their heads. Greedy Gertie grinned and said "Smells great" with her secret hid safe and sound far above her deceitful head.

Chapter Five

The call came late at night. Bubba Doo Wah Wah, a large golden retriever of the Semper Fi Canine Reconnaissance Corps, was sound asleep. In his dream, he was romping through his favorite meadow in Crystal Creek--the one with the sparkling stream and lots of butterflies flitting about the multi-colored fields of swaying flowers. He was hot on the pursuit of a stray cat that had wandered in and he bounded after it like a freight train run off the tracks. He had almost caught up with the feline when...*beep, beep, beep, beep*...

"Bubba, Bubba, come in Sergeant Doo Wah Wah." The shrill loudspeaker voice jolted him awake.

"Yes, sir, Sergeant Bubba Doo Wah Wah reporting, sir."

"We have an emergency, Sergeant. Report at once to Canine Headquarters!"

Groggily, Bubba Doo Wah Wah plopped his face into his water dish to force the sleep out of his head. Shaking it briskly from side to side to awaken himself, he bounded out the door and down the lane to the wooded secret headquarters of the Semper Fi's. He gave the secret bark and General Sedmeyer, a towering as well as fearsome Great Dane, let him in. Already gathered within the secluded room were the top brass, so Bubba knew this had to be serious.

"Gentlemen, we have no time to waste as this is a very serious matter," intoned General Sedmeyer in his most auspicious military voice. "Kenny the Koala Bear, the son of the late Lieutenant Joseph Koala, has been kidnapped." Gasps could be heard throughout the room followed by a shocked hush that only lasted a moment. Then exclamations, one after another: "How, when, where....??!!"

Lieutenant Joseph Koala had been a valiant fighter in the Corps. A bear the caliber of valor then or since had not been seen. Everyone spoke in reverential tones when the tale was told of how Lieutenant Joseph Koala saved his whole platoon and made the ultimate sacrifice by throwing himself upon the grenade that would have ended every creature's life in that platoon. Instead, just one died that fateful day. Everyone in the Crystal Creek animal realm knew about Lieutenant Joseph Koala. His son Kenny was just a baby in his sweet wife Katie's arms when the lieutenant had died for his country. Kenny had never known his father, but the Corps had made it their special mission to be father figures to Kenny when time allowed from their duties, and they would take him on campouts and hikes and tell him wonderful heroic stories about his late father. The Corps all loved Kenny and watched out for him and his mom, Katie. And now this alarming bolt out of the blue.

"Order, order," commanded the General. "I will be commissioning you at once to take on this very serious and potentially dangerous mission. We will also be aligning ourselves with the forces of Puss Puss B' Guss Guss as we not only require canine sensibility but feline stealth and craftiness."

Groans and growls went through the ranks. "Now, I understand, gentlemen, but this is a mission that will require many forces to unite in order to succeed. Our enemy is fierce--but we are stronger. Our strength lies in unity of purpose together with diversity of ability. We will also be utilizing our Rangers--the brave men of the forest to help spy out where Kenny may be hidden."

"Ooh Rah and get busy! Your briefs are contained in these packets. Review them within your unit and be ready to advance at first light."

Kenny the Koala Bear's head ached. That last fall to the floor had been a doozy. And grateful though he was that he no longer smelled like rancid oil and rotten fish, his body felt tender all over from the fierce scrubbing that he had received at the bony hands of Greedy Gertie. The overwhelming noxious fumes of the mothballs was not helping the pounding already going on between his ears. *And, again with the dark? What was this person's fascination with stuffing me into dark, enclosed spaces? At least this time I'm resting on something soft unlike before being banged about like a sack of potatoes being thrown into a bin.*

Laying there in the dark, Kenny began to think about his mother and how worried she must be. *This is just awful--how could I have been so foolish to wander from the borders of our safe home--this must be what she so often warned me about--this terrible land with these horrid, nasty people!*

Kenny had thought it best to be motionless when the Pomposities had been inspecting, prodding and expecting him to move earlier. He realized right away that they could not tell that he was actually an alive bear, <u>not</u> a stuffed one, as they mistook him to be. He felt that this would be to his advantage in the future and perhaps could provide his opportunity for escape when they were not looking. *Surely by now, momma will have contacted the Corps. But, how can they find me when I am locked up in this dark trunk. And, I'm starving!*

All these thoughts were leading to such despair for a bear that had been through entirely too much today. Big tears began forming in his eyes and were soon puddling onto his newly washed fur. The crying made his head hurt more and his tummy to feel the waves of hunger pangs to a greater degree.

Suddenly, a warm, radiating light pierced through the darkness that enveloped Kenny the Koala Bear and rather than striking fear into Kenny's heart, he felt an incredible calm. And peace. Almost like he was totally submerged in it from head to toe. His head immediately stopped throbbing too. He couldn't see where this incredible light was coming from but it was all around him. In the brightness, he saw what looked like cookies in the corner of the trunk and from deep within his being, he heard an inner voice telling him to eat them and that they would satisfy his hunger as well as his thirst. Kenny, the <u>very hungry</u> Koala Bear, wasted no time in doing so as he had enough room to turn over and crawl on his belly to reach them. And it was just as he had been told. His hunger and thirst were instantly gone.

"Who are you? Where are you? Can you get me out of here?"

"Kenny, do you not know me by now? You asked for my help earlier today."

The voice seemed almost audible on the outside of Kenny, but somehow he was being spoken to deep within himself.

"Are you my King?" Kenny ventured with a hushed tone.

"Yes, little koala, I am your King. The one you have turned to every day of your tender life."

Kenny the Koala Bear felt a rush of hope and joy flood his being. "Then, if it is truly you, you can set me free from this place!" exclaimed Kenny.

"Yes, little bear, I can do that, if that is what you desire with all your heart."

"Yes, yes, at once, at once, I do desire this! I want to go home!"

There was a pause and though the light still surrounded Kenny, he sensed a change. Then he heard his King's voice once again.

"Do you truly desire this Kenny, even if doing so would cause you to forfeit fulfilling your mission in life?"

Kenny the Koala Bear was now thoroughly perplexed. "I don't understand, my King. How can my going back home to the momma who loves me be wrong? How could my mission in life be to be trapped in a trunk in a dusty attic?"

The voice was silent for a longer time now and Kenny feared that he had been too outspoken.

"Please my King, I don't mean to be rude, I just don't understand."

The voice was quieter now. More subdued, but with a serious-ness and firmness and truth that gripped Kenny the Koala Bear's entire being.

"Little bear, I cannot explain to you the entire purpose of your special mission which I have created uniquely for you. It would overwhelm you to such a degree that you would let fear grip your heart rather than the faith and love that comes from me in order to carry it out. All I can reveal to you right now is that Today is the day to make this decision. The choice you make will determine whether you are walking in my will for your life or your will. My way is a way of blessing but it is not an easy way and you will face many hardships and trials. My way is one where I will never leave you or forsake you even when you cannot feel my presence. The other way looks easy and at first is full of pleasures and delights. But they soon vanish and all that is left behind is regrets and disappointments. The choice is yours, Kenny. Are you willing to trust me?"

Kenny had been listening intently to his King but this last question pierced his heart. He knew that his King would not lie to him or harm him, but now he was being asked to trust in a plan for his life without knowing where it might lead. And it sounded a little scary, this mission thing. But he also knew from momma's training that the King would never lead anyone who followed Him astray.

Kenny took a deep breath and said from the depth of his heart: "I want your will for my life, my King. Help me to be strong and courageous in following you."

"You already are, young one. You already are."

And with those words the light faded away, but the King's peace remained, covering Kenny like the softest down blanket. Completely relaxed now and enveloped in love, Kenny the Koala Bear sailed off into the sweetest slumber he had ever known hidden still in the trunk of the dusty attic in the Pomposity home.

The barracks were silent as each member of the Semper Fi Canine Reconnaissance Corps opened their briefing packet entitled " The K Mission" and poured through its contents. Sergeant Bubba Doo Wah Wah was a generally happy go lucky type of a fellow, who, in his gallivanting moods, would romp through a house knocking over whatever misplaced lamp that happened to get in the way of his wagging tail. However, once given a mission by the Corps, he was all brass tacks and down to business with a trained nose that could smell out evil in whatever dark corner it lurked in. His wagging tail would then stand straight up at attention and his keen canine eyes would narrow in a see through the nonsense intensity. This was serious business that he was reading now. Kenny the Koala Bear was presumably in danger and he must lead this unit of canines to rescue him.

As he read, his heart ached for a moment as he saw the note of the urgent call that had come into the Corps at 2100 hours from the very frantic Katie Koala. Bubba Doo Wah Wah had a special tender heart for this family as he had been one of the first of the Corps to befriend Kenny when he was just a toddler. Kenny had so taken to Bubba Doo Wah Wah that he was a frequent welcomed visitor by Katie Koala and spent many a free leave time there as a second home. Splashing in and out of the pond to retrieve tennis balls that little Kenny the Koala Bear would throw in toddler squeals of delight had made for many pleasant summer Sunday afternoons. Katie Koala was always very forgiving of their rambunctious play even when a lamp (or two) got broke as they chased one another through the house.

Bubba Doo Wah Wah shook himself. *Enough emotional reminiscing. This is clouding my rational mind. These are long ago memories. Kenny is not a baby any longer. But, just not old enough to keenly recognize danger.*

Bubba looked about as he saw his unit reading the brief. They had about 5 hours 'til first light. "Men, we need to get a bit of shut eye--we will resume at 0500 hours." Growls of agreement reached his ears. Lights snapped off.

Bubba Doo Wah Wah waited the half hour necessary to hear the first snores of old Baggy Bassett (lovingly named due to his droopy eyes). Then, he knew it was safe to silently slink out the flap door of the grey concrete barracks into the still crisp night air. For his personal brief contained this extra information at the end: "Tell no one else in your unit. The following information is for your eyes only. Head as soon as is discreetly possible to Puss Puss B' Guss Guss' house and then onward to Rick the Red-Necked Ranger, the head man of the Rangers in Pine Valley Forest. Give him the enclosed red envelope. Follow what he tells you to do. Your unit will be joining you at 0800 hours at Rick the Red-Necked Ranger's central tower location there."

Bubba Doo Wah Wah moved stealthily and silently across the base staying in the shadows until he reached the underground tunnel entrance located beneath the fake oil barrel bolted to the cement outside the chow hall back door. This secret tunnel was known only to select elite in the Corps. The passage went beneath the entire length of the base and exited into the adjacent woods. The opening to this tunnel was hidden in a hollowed out oak tree and had an element of bark recognition security that opened only to specific members' barks. Once there, Bubba barked the special code and the wood flap swung open as he lunged through. It swung back automatically behind him. He galloped off at top canine speed to Puss Puss B' Guss Guss' house with darkness covering him as a shield.

Chapter Six

The afternoon spent digging in the rich earth of Hannah's mother's garden had definitely calmed Hannah's soul from the earlier afternoon upheaval at the Pomposity home. It was a warm afternoon in spite of it being the fall season and the warmth of the earth as she turned it over with hand-held spade and trowel became a rhythm of praise back to her King for making such a beautiful creation to dwell in. They were digging in a small flowerbed next to the custom built onyx stone waterfall that flowed over the radiantly brilliant, sparkling earth tone boulders into a pond below where fat orange goldfish lived beneath the floating lilies that often hid them from view. A flash of orange every now and again with quick little splashes betrayed their hidden fishy presence. The multi-colored rose bushes surrounding the pond had given their last bloom for the summer and had been trimmed back last weekend in preparation for the upcoming colder months. But today, it was so gorgeously warm that it was almost like spring, and Hannah had heard her mom and dad talking at the breakfast table that it was supposed to be like this throughout the weekend. As Hannah plunged another tulip bulb into the rich earth, a wonderful idea came across her mind.

"Momma, when daddy comes home tonight, can we pack up the car and go for a campout in the Pine Valley Forest? I haven't seen Uncle Rick in awhile and I would really like to go up in his lookout tower to see all the pretty trees that are changing colors. And we could cook some hamburgers and hot dogs out tonight--and make s'mores and tell stories around the campfire...and..."

"Whoa, slow down my adventure seeker! I don't know if your father would want to do that tonight or not--he may have work to do tomorrow. I'll have to see when he gets home."

"Oh, momma, call him now, please! Then, we could have everything ready to go when he gets home and we could just take off right away while it's still light--please, momma, please?"

Judith looked at those excited eyes that only an hour before had been so sad. "Well, my love," she said wiping her dirt encrusted hands on her knees and standing to her feet, "If you will finish planting these last few bulbs, I will go in and get my cell phone and call your dad."

"Thank you, momma." As Judith Stillwaters neared the sliding door to the family room, Hannah added, "And remind daddy that this could be our last campout 'til next summer!"

The drive to Pine Valley Forest was only about an hour. The roads were softly winding and a beatific scenic trip at this time of year. Yellows, golds, crimson, burnt orange--a panoramic color explosion greeted the eyes on both sides of the road as one traveled along the two lane to the heart of the most lush pine grove in the county. Hannah nestled happily in the back seat next to her purple and yellow sleeping bag. Several thick plaid blankets surrounded the nearby ice chest, filled to the brim with the hamburger meat and hot dogs together with the bacon and eggs for morning fare. Behind the driver's seat on the floor were the bags containing chips, pickles, and beef jerky as well as marshmallows, graham crackers and chocolate bars to make s'mores. Hannah's pleas for a final season overnight campout cookout had actually been quite the welcome respite call to Daniel Stillwaters who was work weary from the indoor office week grind. Upon arriving home, he had wasted no time in changing from his business suit to faded blue jeans, flannel shirt and boots. To Hannah, he was handsome in whatever he wore and in her book, the most wonderful, loving father in the world. But, boy, could he sing off key! Which he was doing right now in a rousing rendition of "She'll be coming round the mountain when she comes" as they came up to the main dirt road turnoff that would lead them to a campsite not too far from her Uncle Rick's main lookout tower.

Uncle Rick was the other special man in Hannah's world. He was her favorite uncle, her mother's brother. The folk of Crystal Creek affectionately dubbed him Rick the Red-Necked Ranger because he also had that outdoor, hard work earned, sun-kissed red neck from all the time he spent in the great outdoors of Pine Valley Forest. Hannah had loved going camping in this forest ever since she could remember, as far back as her fourth birthday, although mom and dad told her they started camping with her there when she had just turned two. The family always felt safe with Uncle Rick just less than a half mile down a soft, pine needle path from their favorite campsite. Rick spoiled Hannah too with everything he could from homemade rocking horses to hand carved toy benches to unique wood whistles that he carved and whittled from the fallen trees of the forest. They were made into shapes resembling everything from zoo animals to miniature cabins to one specially designed for Hannah's mom on her birthday with roses up and down the stem. Each whistle had its own unique sound to accompany its special shape. Rick never sold them although he could have as they were of such fine quality and workmanship. No, he delighted in giving them as gifts to the town folk of Crystal Creek and many a sick child had been happily cheered during a hospital stay with this thoughtful gift from the red-necked ranger.

But his most prized gift to Hannah had been that of Puss Puss B' Guss Guss when Hannah turned six. He had even custom built the blue carpet, kitty tree/scratcher/climbing house that resided in Hannah's room for this fluffy feline that had stolen Hannah's heart the moment she saw him. Judith thought it was way too expensive a pet for such a young girl, but, she adored cats as well. Puss Puss B' Guss Guss with his soft fur, gentle demeanor, and puppy dog like attachment even won over Daniel Stillwaters' heart. Daniel would have preferred a family dog, but, sadly, he was highly allergic to dog dander. When Puss Puss followed him around on the weekends like a puppy, he declared that this pet was the best of both the canine and feline worlds--a cat who behaved like a dog and who he didn't have to take out for a bathroom stroll at 3 A.M.

"Here we are, gang," dad's singing broken by his joyful exclamation. The car had made its final turn and now was rolling to a halt at their old familiar campsite. As Hannah fairly exploded out the backseat car door, the scent of the huge pine trees towering overhead greeted and filled her senses. Dad popped open the trunk to reveal the large family tent, lawn chairs and his portable charcoal grill that always accompanied every camping venture. Daniel was the "charcoal king" as his family had lovingly nicknamed him as he relished the fair weather seasons and utilized them at every opportunity to grill anything and everything that could possibly go on a grill from meats to vegetables to even fruits. And, it was all so delicious! Hannah's friends loved being invited to the Stillwaters' summer grill fests.

"Did you bring the salt and pepper and garlic powder?" queried dad as he carried the grill to a trusty clear spot to get the charcoal going while momma and Hannah set the groceries on the picnic table.

"Yes, dear, they're in the sack with the spatulas and silverware."

Daniel Stillwaters already had the coals poured, arranged by hand into a triangle mound, and lighter fluid immersed when Judith's answer came. With a fiery *whoosh*, the coals were aflame. Just twenty minutes away from plopping those juicy burgers onto the grill and a few precious minutes' worth of intense charcoal grilling later would give birth to biting into the best tasting burgers this side of the Rio Grande! The hot dogs would then be carefully arranged and in a few minutes time, they would have that blackened outer crispness that his family loved. Daniel smiled to himself as this outdoor setting always brought forth a secret cowboy, rugged adventure heart, a far cry from his sedentary work-a-day office life. His ride away into the sunset thoughts on his imaginary steed, Bronco, were interrupted by: "Daddy, can I go down the trail to see if Uncle Rick is up in his ranger tower?"

"No, sweetie, by the time you got there, these burgers will be done and the sun will be setting soon after. Tell you what, though, first thing after breakfast in the morning, and we'll all head up there to surprise your Uncle Rick." Daniel tussled his daughter's fair colored locks with fatherly affection. "In the meantime, why don't you help your mom get that picnic table set with all the goodies we'll need to go with your dad's famous cowboy burgers and blackened dogs?"

Judith had already shaken out the well-worn and beloved red and white checkered picnic tablecloth and was busily covering its surface with paper plates, plastic silverware, napkins and other necessary picnic fare. "Hannah, could you bring me the sack from behind the driver's seat? I need to get the chips and dip ready."

Momma always made the best French onion dip--perfect accompaniment to dad's burgers and hot dogs. "Oh, and bring the pickles and olives too."

"Judith, did you bring any corn?" asked Hannah's dad. He made the best corn on the cob grilled in the husks over the coals.

"Hannah--the corn is in the other sack. Take it to your dad right away."

Hannah felt a bit like a yo-yo running back and forth to the car for each new request from mom or dad--but, truthfully, she really didn't mind because being here in this beautiful forest brought such peace and joy to Hannah's heart. This was life at its best for Hannah--being outside in the crisp, pine scented air, dad with that relaxed and boyish look on his face as smoke came up in clouds as burgers sizzled, mom merrily cutting up fresh fruit and setting the table like a royal palace banquet and she, Hannah, being a part of their love and playful bantering back and forth. All of this gave Hannah the same feeling as a cozy blanket nestled around her watching the roaring fire on a cold winter's night in their home in Crystal Creek. Safety, security and serenity surrounded her with a warmth like the melted butter soon to be dripping over those ears of blackened corn. As they sat around the table saying grace before digging in to their bountiful feast, Hannah sent up a silent request to her King for her life to always feel this deep serenity that she felt clothed in right now for the rest of her days.

Now with tummies filled with charred hot dogs, cowboy burgers, corn on the cob, chips and dip, pickles, olives and fruit salad, the last rays of light were filtering through the tall pines as the Stillwaters family hurriedly pitched the family tent, unrolled sleeping bags and blankets and placed flashlights near each pillow. The campsite outhouse was not too far away, but without a flashlight, it would be easy to become disoriented in the dark forest. The first twinkle of Venus poked through the darkening sky beyond the ridge and the coal embers were perfect for the delightful ritual of s'mores before settling in for the night. The wood had been too damp to make the campfire that Hannah had hoped for, but that first bit of gooey chocolate, sticky burnt marshmallow and graham cracker goodness wiped any trace of disappointment far from Hannah's mind.

With faces and hands rinsed from their five-gallon plastic water container, they took turns changing into fleece for the night's slumber. Dad was quite entertaining with a story of the two eagles who couldn't decide where to go on vacation, complete with his silly voices and flashlight antics. The last thing that Hannah remembered hearing was her mom's soft voice telling a story of a young Indian girl who took a canoe downstream to visit her cousin who lived in a village far away. As the girl sailed away to see her cousin, Hannah too sailed away into deep restful sleep in their tent beneath the pines.

Chapter Seven

Bubba Doo Wah Wah was one of the fastest runners in the Semper Fi Canine Reconnaissance Corps. He had been at the top of his class since boot camp and he was often chosen as he made his way up in ranks to lead P.T. He stayed fit with a daily routine of exercise and a high protein diet. Tonight, all of his physical training was faring him well as he stealthily sped along the silent dark streets of Crystal Creek to Puss Puss B' Guss Guss' house. He had no idea how he was going to rouse Puss Puss without alerting his human owners, but he belonged to the Corps, the elite of all the fighting forces, and one thing true, trained Corps dogs know well, is how to improvise.

Rounding the last corner, Bubba Doo Wah Wah sloshed through an unexpected mud puddle in the yard next to Puss Puss B' Guss Guss' house. The twin three-year-old girls who lived there had made quite the muddy mess earlier that day. He hit it with such a galloping force that it coated his underbelly and his four paws were covered with the gloppy earth. It startled him for an instant, but Bubba went forward with characteristic determination that only the Corps training could engender. Purpose. Mission. Singleness of mind. Force out all distractions contrary to such.

The house was dark as he approached save for a solitary porch light. Bubba stayed close to the front hedges to avoid any possibility of detection. He knew that Puss Puss B' Guss Guss' window faced the street so he would have to make sure that he remained in the shadows. First, a bit of surveillance was necessary to secure his position.

Bubba Doo Wah Wah peered through a break in the bushes to make absolutely certain no one was up and about. He looked right. Quiet as a mouse. The streetlights and porch lights were the only lights on save the silvery crescent moon high in the sky--too small to provide any light for the earth below. He peered left towards the garage and driveway. Now here was something to take note of. The garage door was down (as usual at this time of night for Bubba had made other trips here in the past) but there was something missing in the driveway. There was always a van parked there, but tonight, there was none. Bubba's pulse quickened and elated thoughts began racing through his lightning quick canine mind. *Perhaps this is my lucky night! Possibly the owners are gone which would mean Puss Puss is alone and my mission to get him and take him with me will now be exceedingly easy with no owners to accidentally awaken! Steady now, boy--still must proceed with caution just in case there is another reason for the missing van.*

Bubba left his peering through the bush post and stretched his front quarters forward towards the house and the brick ledge beneath Puss Puss' window and tapped ever so gently with his muddy paw on the glass. Three taps and a pause. Three taps and a pause. Three taps and a pause. And then two loud barks. And then repeated. This was the well-known signal to Puss Puss B' Guss Guss. Once completed, Bubba Doo Wah Wah hid in the bushes to avoid discovery by anyone who might have stirred. With sharp, trained canine eyes, he stared transfixed at the window awaiting that sly feline's appearance or responding mew.

Just as he thought he would have to repeat the process, he saw the curtain rustle and that white fluffy feline's head pushed aside the curtain and peered out in the night. This was always a fun part of any mission as Bubba Doo Wah Wah, in playful glee in order to startle the Puss Puss, jumped up and stuck his face against the glass. Puss Puss B' Guss Guss hissed and raised a paw against the window swatting vigorously at him against the glass. Bubba could tell from the expressions and *meowrs* that Puss Puss was <u>not</u> amused. But, it was worth it to see his fur stand up, back arched, ears battened back attempting to look fierce. Priceless. He knew he would hear about it soon enough when Puss Puss B' Guss Guss made his way down the secret hollow interior of the indoor cat tower that Rick the Red-Necked Ranger had made and would exit soon from the wine barrel planter with the hidden empty bottom.

From outward appearance, the wine barrel looked normal but it too had been secretly engineered by Rick. The top half was a normal barrel planter filled with dirt and the multi-colored flowers that Judith Stillwaters lovingly attended. Her gift of a green thumb showed forth in the bountiful array that bloomed from spring to fall. The wine barrel was cemented to the sidewalk but the bottom third was open inside and the tunnel from the kitty tree exited into this space. There was a small door hinged on the inside that blended into the rest of the wood on the barrel appearing as though there was no break in the wood and meow activated to Puss Puss B' Guss Guss' particular feline pitch.

Bubba Doo Wah Wah stood a ways back just in case Puss Puss B' Guss Guss emerged with claws flaring. He had received the sting of those sharp razors once on his tender canine snout and he was not about to experience it a second time. The little, wine-barrel kitty door swung open and Puss Puss B' Guss Guss emerged, with white fur a muss and a glare in his sky blue eyes.

"This had better be good, dog, to wake me in the wee hours."

"Puss Puss, we have no time to waste. We have to get to Pine Valley Forest by sun up for a meeting of the Corps."

"Isn't that a matter strictly for you drool jowls--what has this to do with us felines--and why the Forest?"

"Puss Puss--this is serious! The Rangers are being called into this. I cannot tell you more until we convene in the forest. Please don't make this difficult."

Puss Puss could tell from Bubba's tone that this was no joke. Something serious was a foot to get this canine so riled.

"Are your owners at home?"

"No, they went on some kind of trip for the night--heard them saying they would be back tomorrow evening."

"Well--no time to waste then--I will have you back before they return--hop aboard!"

Bubba got down on his belly to enable Puss Puss B' Guss Guss to jump up onto his back and to burrow down in the pack secured there. A small blanket was inside for the Puss Puss to nestle in which served the dual purpose of keeping the fur ball secure and preventing his well sharpened claws from piercing through the backpack material into Bubba's back. Puss Puss obliged Bubba's urgency and settled deep within the pack; with a meow and a bark, they raced off into the night towards Pine Valley Forest. It would be a three-hour long journey. The bouncing and regular cadence of this golden retriever, Bubba Doo Wah Wah, soon lulled Puss Puss B' Guss Guss back into kitty dreamland.

The first rays of morning light shown through the tent flap causing Hannah to rouse from her deep slumber. The pine air always had the same wonderful effect on her--a restful, peaceful slumber from which she didn't wake until dawn. At home, Puss Puss B' Guss Guss' jumping on the bed would often disturb her sleep but she usually could go back to her dreams. Up here, she could never remember any dreams so sound was her sleep.

Hannah peered into the other side of the tent. This was a large, two-room camping tent which gave plenty of privacy and space. Dad was snoring away and momma's slow deep breathing seemed to provide a harmony to dad's rhythm. Hannah decided not to disturb their rest.

She unzipped her side of the tent and poked her head outside. A bit chilly, but she knew her fleece lined, denim jacket with her tur-tleneck sweater would keep her warm. She hurriedly dressed, mostly inside her sleeping bag in order to keep the morning chill at bay. With a final lace up of her trusty hiking boots and a last tug on her bright pink stocking cap to keep her ears nice and toasty, Hannah was set for the day's adventure.

As she stepped out of the tent, she noticed the most gorgeous blue jay she had ever seen perched in a tree whose branch was just above the picnic table where they had enjoyed such a feast last night. Hannah attempted to stay motionless in order to not frighten it away. It flitted about on the branch turning its deep blue head this way and that. Then, off he flew on the breeze of this delightful morning to explore new territory.

Hannah felt as restless as the blue jay. The fresh crisp air made it difficult to be still. *Mom and dad will probably not be up for another hour yet to start breakfast,* she reasoned. She fished into her jacket pocket for her note pad and pen that were always a mainstay of her wardrobe for Hannah loved to write things down as she felt inspired to do so. *I'll leave a note letting them know I'm just down the trail at Uncle Rick's Ranger Tower,* she thought. With that resolve, Hannah wrote the note placing it securely beneath a rock in the center of the picnic table. Feeling frisky as Puss Puss B' Guss Guss with a new catnip mouse toy, Hannah took off along the pine needle trail in a gait between a skip and a run.

Through the clearing, a slightly winded Bubba Doo Wah Wah could see his unit gathering about the base of the central tower manned by Rick the Red-Necked Ranger. There were 44 in all; breeds of every kind, selected specifically for this top secret mission to rescue Kenny the Koala Bear from whatever unknown forces had absconded with him. Each canine had different skills and abilities that put together, would surely roust out the enemy and defeat him. For starters, there was Lance Corporal James, the brown and white beagle, who had a nose that could sniff a sock from 300 paces away. Private First Class Roy, the greyhound, affectionately called the Galloping Gazelle, could run up to 43 miles an hour. Corporal Sherman, the St. Bernard, once carried a young child for more than a mile through two feet of snow in blizzard conditions. These were just a few of the more than 40 skills exemplified in this unit.

Bubba Doo Wah Wah had yet to be in a special mission assignment wherein they had not come back victorious. Now that Kenny's very life could be at stake...*well, there was just no acceptable outcome other than a triumphant one.* Bubba's serious contemplation changed to physical pain--"OW!" Watch those claws, Puss Puss!" as the pampered, but very bright feline poked his head out of the backpack to get a better view.

"Don't you dare put me down in this dirt. I am not going to spend two hours licking red dirt dust out of this white silk of mine."

"Don't worry, fuss budget--just maintain your perch without killing me with those needle claws, all right?!"

With that admonition, Bubba bounded down the hill towards his men. As he drew near, he spied Rick making his descent down the steep ladder of the massive central tower. Bubba had great affection for this ranger as Rick had raised him from a scrawny pup when he found him abandoned in these very woods. He had grown to adult doghood around the special breed of men called the Rangers and he loved and respected these men for the hard and tireless work they did as agents of protection for both human and animal kind. They had the unique gifting of being able to understand all types of languages--both human and animal. However, this was not a fact known to the population at large. Only those who encountered the Rangers were aware that they understood their tongue. The population at large knew nothing about their interaction with the animal realm. This was privileged information that was well guarded for protection of their various missions.

When Bubba had reached maturity, Rick had brought him to the Semper Fi Canine Reconnaissance Corps and he had loved it from day one, just as Rick had known he would. Many a mission had been carried out to successful fruition, but none so important or with so much emotion attached to it as this one.

"Puss Puss, get that red sealed envelope out of the side pocket of the pack."

"What, I'm now the mail man?" quipped Puss Puss.

"Just do it," Bubba growled.

"O.k., o.k., don't get your drooly drawers in a wad!" Puss Puss deftly reached in the pocket and stuck a sharp claw nail through the opening where it was not completely sealed. It fell out at Bubba's feet where he carefully grasped it in his teeth just as Rick the Red-Necked Ranger reached the ground and spun around.

"Hey, old buddy!" Rick came leaping forward and flung his arms around Bubba Doo Wah Wah's neck. He never treated Bubba with any military formality like he did the other canines. His respect ran deep nonetheless. "What have you got for me this time? Oh, a <u>red</u> envelope--must be a serious one."

Rick took the envelope from Bubba's jowls and while he read it in silence, Bubba took his place in front of his unit and called them to attention, awaiting the instructions of this rugged ranger. After a long silence, Rick's strong and loud voice filled the clearing.

"Men of the Semper Fi Canine Reconnaissance Corps: Kenny the Koala Bear has been abducted by forces as yet unknown. We have very little to go on at this point in time, so, we have to assume and explore every possibility from both a civilian and military perspective, while keeping this under the radar until we narrow the potentialities of what group is responsible for this bear's disappearance. He was last seen playing in the eucalyptus grove by a neighbor of Katie Koala at 1400 hours yesterday. Most of you know Kenny well enough to know that he would never run away from his wonderful home and loving mother."

Barks of agreement loudly filled the forest clearing at that last statement.

"His mother has searched their property and thus far, no physical evidence has been obtained to give us a clue as to what transpired. Thus, under the specific orders of General Sedmeyer contained in this envelope, I will be dividing you into six teams with seven men to each team. As there are 44 of you, the extra two that have been specially selected by the General will work directly with me and Sgt. Bubba Doo Wah Wah. The General has given me further instructions to meet with the Koala Bear Unit of the Corps tomorrow in order to engage them to search the rural and forest grove areas surrounding Crystal Creek."

"And you, Puss Puss B' Guss Guss..." At the mention of his name, Puss Puss tentatively poked his head out of the backpack. He did not at all like being in the presence of so many smelly as well as slobbery canines. "You are responsible for rallying and organizing the feline forces, both indoor and outdoor, as well as wild alley cats, to be on the lookout both on the streets and in the homes of Crystal Creek for anything that could lead us to the whereabouts of our Kenny."

At the mention of feline assistance, there were growls and groans and Puss Puss battened back his ears. "Silence, men!" bellowed the Ranger. "Listen up! I will call out the six team captains' names. As I do so, please come forward to receive your written instructions on what section of Crystal Creek or surrounding areas you have been assigned to as well as the list of who will be in your group. Move quickly into your teams next to your leader and review your orders."

One by one, Rick the Red-Necked Ranger intoned the platoon captains' names and the respective captains gathered with their group in the damp forest clearing. Two canines were left: Lance Corporal James the beagle and Corporal Gerald, the German shepherd. The Ranger motioned them to step forward. "The two of you will be with Sgt. Bubba Doo Wah Wah and me."

As the teams were forming, the camaraderie barks filled the area and began echoing through the still early morning forest. Hannah had been walking for about 30 minutes and was almost to the top of the path's last upward turn before descending to the clearing below where it would be an easy run down the hill to Uncle Rick's tower. All that had greeted her ears to this point were the sounds of the Pine Warblers singing their early greet the day songs and an occasional squirrel scampering through the fallen leaves and pine needles of the forest floor. *What was this?* The sound so startled her it caused her to stop in her tracks. *Barking that sounded like a hundred dogs at once! Out here in the woods? Impossible!* Then, as abruptly as the sound had pierced the morning air, it stopped. Hannah began walking, slowly and gently this time, and veered quietly off the path to hide in the trees.

She continued her ascent until she was at the top of the hill, but here, the growth was really too thick to see through. Hannah began searching about for a tree that would have low enough limbs that she could hoist herself up in to obtain a better view before going back to the open path. *If there are wild dogs about, I certainly don't want to be exposed where I might be easy prey for an attack,* she reasoned.

Hannah was quite a good tree climber and had never fallen out of one. She used to scare her grandpa when she was only five years old climbing way up high on the large sturdy limbs of the backyard Mulberry tree . Grandpa would go running in the house to tell her mom to come out and get Hannah down out of that tree "before she breaks her neck" and she would climb down at momma's pleadings so as not to worry dear grandpa. My, how she loved the smell of his pipe tobacco in that yellow pouch tucked in his front shirt pocket (a vice that eventually caused his demise by the time she was seven). He always had a story and a piece of bubblegum for her in his other pocket. These happy memories rambled through her mind as she scoured the top of the hill for a suitable tree.

Ah ha! There's one that looks like it will do. Hannah grasped hold of the lowest branch and swung herself up onto its limb. It was a fairly large tree with lots of branches within easy reach as she climbed from one to the next and then a bit higher. Finally, she could see the sky from her vantage point where she could scan the clearing below.

What an unforeseen spectacle greeted her now big as saucer eyes. Lots and lots of dogs! In many different groups. All barking at one another like they were having some kind of a book club discussion. Hannah pulled herself to a higher, thinner branch for a better view. Now she could see Uncle Rick's tower and...*why, that was Uncle Rick down there with four dogs around him, one of which looked like it had a white cat poking out of a pack on his back.* Hannah rubbed her eyes in disbelief. *This can't be possible!* She was about to holler out to Uncle Rick to let him know she was up here, when she heard him bellow out in his deep booming voice: "You are now commissioned--onward to rescue Kenny the Koala Bear !!!"

At that utterance, all the dogs began a furious barking. The dog with the pack on its back rose up on his hindquarters, dumping the white cat out of the pack sideways to the ground. *Why, that looks just like my Puss Puss---impossible!* Hannah edged further out on the branch for a clearer view not noticing that it was getting dangerously thin the further she ventured out.

"Uncle Rick--Puss Puss? Uncle Rick!" she shouted with all her might. The dogs now went silent. "Uncle Rick! Puss Puss? Uncle Rick!!"

Rick the Red-Necked Ranger as well as Puss Puss B' Guss Guss turned their gaze upward towards that familiar voice just as the horrifying sound of a splitting, cracking branch echoed outward together with Hannah's screams of terror as she fell to the leafy ground below. Then, the worst sound of all. Silence.

Chapter Eight

The pizza had been delicious. Salena the Shrieker loved pizza nights. The Pomposity family had devoured their large sausage with the works pizza in the formal dining room to avoid looking at the disaster of the playroom and living room, which would have been their unsettling view if they had eaten at the informal kitchen table. Pugnacious Pomposity, III hated disorder of any type so the serene dining room with the elegant cherry wood table and matching china cabinet displaying all of Greedy Gertie's prized china treasures afforded a soothing atmosphere in which to have a peaceful dinner to end a most unsettling and chaotic day. During bath time, Salena asked to see the koala bear before going to bed, but, Greedy Gertie simply stated that the bear had been cleaned and put away for the evening and she would just have to wait for another day to see him. Actually, Greedy Gertie had no intention of doing so, but, she was so adept at lying that Salena believed her. Even though Gertie's original thought had been to have this be a present for the children, her covetous nature had taken over once more, and she could not even entertain the thought of sharing her unique find with anyone--not even her children. Thus, Salena's pleas were promptly hushed as Gertie tucked her into bed. Pugnacious Pomposity, III was taking care of putting Horatio the Horrible to bed down the hall as Gertie hollered a brusque "Good night, Horatio" from a distance before retiring herself to their richly ornate master bedroom suite.

As Pugnacious Pomposity, III entered the room to see his wife already with her bedside lamp out, he stated: "Gertie, tomorrow you must call the carpet cleaners to come and remove from our formerly pristine carpet that wretched oily stain left by the raggedy bear as well as the now set-in tea stains spilled from Salena's teapot. My gracious, Gertie, are you not supervising the children properly when I am at work? You know our rules about the living room! Yet, upon my arrival home tonight, I found you with the children in that very room that you know is reserved solely for adults in order to avoid mishaps of this very nature from taking place. What has gotten in to you lately, Gertie?! Are you listening to me?"

Greedy Gertie had been lying on her side with her back to her husband during this whole speech. Gertie had learned that attempting to argue with Pugnacious Pomposity, III was a useless, wasted effort. It didn't matter <u>what</u> the subject was. He was always right and made sure that whoever he was in disagreement with knew this to be so. Even when he was wrong, he was right. So, to avoid further conflict, Gertie pretended to be asleep, letting loose a few gentle fake snores into the room to emphasize this fact.

"Oh, bother," Pugnacious Pomposity, III responded. "She hasn't heard a word I have said. As usual." Resolved to the futility of it all, he undid his dark blue silk robe, placing it most carefully atop the mahogany hope chest at the foot of their bed for morning use and slid off his slippers in precise formation right next to the night table. With a deep exasperated sigh, he flipped off his side nightstand light, crawled beneath the fine Egyptian cotton sheets, and mumbled a disgruntled "good night" to the fake sleeper lying next to him. *Tomorrow will be better, at least I can hope for the best*, he thought as he closed his eyes. *When I arrive at my office tomorrow there will definitely be a soothing order to look forward to*, was the last thought on his mind before slumber overtook Pugnacious Pomposity, III's conscious mind.

The morning light streaming through the open bedroom curtains awakened Greedy Gertie. *What time is it? Seems later than usual.* She glanced at the alarm clock next to the bed. *Good heavens! It was already 8:00!* Turning over, she realized Pugnacious had already left for work as he left precisely at 7:20 every morning of the week and only took Sundays off.

Well, one less person to have to make breakfast for, which considering Gertie's lack of fondness for cooking was a bright thought to begin the day with. *Wonder if my brats are up yet?* The children had no real schedule and weren't allowed to go to school as Pugnacious Pomposity, III had decided before they were even born that <u>he</u> would school his children. He chose to do so not based on any moral or spiritual convictions but solely on the belief that no one was as smart as himself and he wanted his children to know that they were smarter and more elite than the rest of the world. As Greedy Gertie was not the brightest bulb in the box, Pugnacious only allowed her to give the children the appropriate workbooks that he would leave for them with their daily assignments outlined and then when he arrived home, he would personally tutor them. This arrangement perfectly suited Gertie as she saw the whole task as one big bore.

Greedy Gertie slipped on her lime green, Chantilly lace robe and fuzzy slippers, and shuffled out to the kitchen to see if the children were up. The remnants of yesterday's chaos were still strewn about the playroom and living room. Pugnacious Pomposity, III had left a detailed note on the counter for Greedy Gertie as to who to call for the carpet clean up. Gertie was glad that this was Saturday for her maid was due to be here by 9:00 a.m. *Let her deal with this mess, that's what she's paid for.*

No sign of the children yet. *Good.* A few minutes of peace. She poured herself a cup of coffee from the coffeepot that had been left on by Pugnacious and sat down at the kitchen table to drink it. Her thoughts turned to the koala bear in the cedar chest up in the attic. *Wonder if I'll have time to look at him before they get up?* No sooner had that reflection crossed her brain than the sudden realization that in all the hustle and commotion of yesterday, she had quite forgotten where she had put the key to the trunk. She knew for certain that she hadn't returned it to the dresser as the children and her husband had arrived home just as her feet hit the floor from the attic. As she sat sipping her coffee in deep contemplation of where she might have stashed this blasted key, the high-pitched scream of Salena the Shrieker pierced the air so startling Greedy Gertie that she spilled some of her coffee onto her lap. If not for her fuzzy thick robe, this would have hurt; but instead, it was just downright irritating. Exasperated, she grabbed the napkins to blot the coffee color from her lime green robe while hollering in anger, "What are you yelling about, Salena?!" as she shuffled from the kitchen down the hall to the bedroom. It did not take long to find out who was responsible for all this commotion for there stood Horatio laughing hysterically while dangling a rubber hairy tarantula over the headboard of Salena's bed.

Greedy Gertie yanked him from behind the headboard and gave him a sound thwack on the behind accompanied by a shrill "Go to your room--right now!" Away he ran, his former gleeful laughter changed to a whimper. Salena was still shrieking and Gertie's head was starting to throb from too much early morning commotion.

"Come now, Salena, please stop. It was just a fake spider--not real at all. Come with me. Let's go get a doughnut in the kitchen. Some of your favorites: the ones with sprinkles and pink icing!" At the mention of the favorite doughnuts, Salena's shrieking lessened and she climbed down off her bed to follow mother Gertie to the kitchen.

"Here you go." Gertie placed the luscious pink strawberry iced doughnut with multi-colored sprinkles in front of Salena as she hopped up onto the stool at the kitchen countertop. As Greedy Gertie was pouring the milk into Salena the Shrieker's special Fanny the Fairy Princess cup, the front doorbell chime rang.

"Is this ever grand central station this morning!" fumed Gertie, setting Salena's glass in front of her.

"I'll get it!" hollered Horatio the Horrible who had quickly recovered from his earlier disgrace. He came bursting out of his room at a full gallop and slid the rest of the way, as was his custom, in dirty, stocking feet into the front door before Greedy Gertie even reached the hall. Gertie's call for Horatio to wait before opening the door was ignored in his zeal to discover what new face could be on the other side of the ornately carved, cherry wood door. Once flung open, however, Horatio yelled with disappointment and a tinge of arrogance learned from his father: "Just the maid," and he took off running back to his room to avoid momma Gertie's inevitable anger.

Matilda was a simple woman--unassuming and pleasant. Her English was not very good which posed nary a problem as she had not been hired by the Pomposities for her communication skills but simply for her cleaning abilities. Pugnacious Pomposity, III was the one who did the hiring and had gone through a string of prior maids due to Greedy Gertie's tendencies towards temper fits as well as the children's unruliness. Thus, Matilda had only been with them for about a month and her lack of comprehension in the English language department was turning out to be an asset rather than a disadvantage for the Pomposity household.

Greedy Gertie had now made it to the entryway with the exclamation of "You're here early this morning", which was met by just a nod and smile from Matilda. "There's quite a mess from yesterday," Gertie continued on waving her arms towards the living room and gesturing towards the playroom with Matilda trailing behind her. "Start in these two rooms while I go get dressed. I have to call the carpet cleaners." Off Gertie went to her room with Matilda left to her cleaning devices in the living room.

Salena the Shrieker hopped off the kitchen stool, strawberry iced doughnut, now half-eaten and still in hand, to make her presence known to Matilda. Salena really liked Matilda as she found her lilting accent to be both fascinating and soothing to her soul. So much of Salena's world was filled with angry shouts and taunting words as well as her own shrill shrieking in response to the above that Matilda's soft-spoken tones and cheerful laughter brought a note of hope and peace so hungered for to this little girl's world.

Salena peered around the corner of the wall into the living room and was delighted to catch Matilda's eye which caused her to give a smile as big as sunshine in Salena's direction. Salena smiled back and then scurried to the corner of the kitchen to grab momma Gertie's apron off the hook so that she could put it on and prance after Matilda pretending to clean in imitation of the expert. Matilda never minded and Salena the Shrieker truly enjoyed the Saturday clean about.

"Tie me please, Matilda," Salena said as she struggled with the apron's bow. Soon the two were in motion like the melody and harmony of an orchestrated piece of music: Matilda this way and she that with the happy effect of disorder gradually transforming into order erasing yesterday's tornado-like devastation from the playroom and living room. The only tell-tale evidence left on the otherwise lily white living room carpet were the ugly brown tea stains, the rather large, oily circle where Kenny had been dumped onto the carpet, and a smaller circle near the coffee table where he had been propped against its leg. As Matilda left the straightened living room to concentrate on the mopping of the kitchen, Salena the Shrieker started twirling and jumping about the long living room pretending she was a famous ballerina. Momma Gertie's apron billowed out around her as she did her leaps and spins. Her last pirouette sent her a little too close to the tall mahogany chest/bookcase at the far end of the room and as the apron flew out as she twirled, it came in contact with the wood and a tiny clang sound was heard. As Salena bumped into the chest, she saw a small, glittery piece of metal fly out of the front apron pocket, bounce on the carpet and land behind the overstuffed armchair.

As she crawled behind the chair to see what had flown out of the apron, she heard the doorbell ring and Horatio's bedroom door bang open again with his "I'll get it cry" ringing loud and clear through the house. As Salena the Shrieker peered under the corner of the chair nearest to the wall, she spied what she had been looking for and reached her small fingers around its unusual shape. Just as she grasped it, she heard her mother's high heel clatter in the entryway and angry voice yelling at Horatio to get away from the door. She shoved this small metal object quickly into her blue jean pocket and hurriedly came out into the living room so as not to be asked what she was doing back there.

She exited just in time to see momma Gertie push Horatio away from the front door and open it to a man who announced that he was with the Cool Klean Carpet Service. As equipment, men and machine came into the home, Greedy Gertie called the children into the playroom.

"Now, children, I have to go the grocery store. I won't be gone that long."

"Why can't we come with you?" pleaded Salena.

"You can't," said Gertie, "because Matilda is still here and will be cleaning until noon and the carpet cleaning men will also be here for a couple of hours to get our living room carpet back to normal. What I expect from you two is to stay off the carpet and out of their way. Matilda is in charge of you and if you don't mind, you won't get to enjoy the special dessert treat I am bringing home for after dinner tonight. And, Horatio, if you are mean to your sister, you won't have any dinner <u>or</u> dessert tonight, do you understand?" This last remark was said with a glare piercingly turned in Horatio's direction that would have made a snake retreat in fear.

"Yes, ma'am," sighed Horatio as his stomach always won out over his desire to torment his sister. When momma Gertie promised a special dessert treat from the store, it was definitely <u>not</u> something that he wanted to miss out on for mischievous behavior as she always brought home extraordinarily great desserts!

"O.k., now--then that's settled. Matilda!" she bellowed as she clattered out of the playroom to the bedroom hallway where the whirr of Matilda's vacuuming was now in full force. The children heard it stop for a moment and Greedy Gertie's muffled instructions with a loud "Be back soon" and a solid bang of the garage entry door. The whirr of the vacuum resumed.

"You look really goofy with that apron on," teased Horatio. "Why don't you take it off so we can go out back and play kickball?"

"I don't look goofy," said Salena. "And I don't want to play kickball. Besides, I found something really neat in this apron."

"What?" What did you find? Show me!"

"Why should I?" You'll just take it away. It's mine 'cause I found it."

"Aww, come on Salena. Show me! This is boring just sitting around. If you show me, I'll play whatever game you want."

"Whatever game? Even with my dolls?"

This made Horatio pause for a moment. He hated dolls, but he was so bored. Now that his curiosity was aroused, he needed to find out what Salena had found.

"Yes, all right--but only for a little while. Come on now--show me what you found!"

Salena reached deep into her front jean pocket and felt again the odd-shaped metal object that she herself had not had a chance to get a good look at. She now brought it forth, placing it into her left palm so they could both look at it more closely.

"Why--it's a really old key! Looks like it would fit a pirate's treasure chest!" exclaimed Horatio. The key was about three inches long and tarnished bronze in color. At one end, it sported three prongs--two long and one short. The opposite end was clover leaf-shaped with fancy scrolling wrapped around each leaf. The shaft portion of the key had delicately carved flowers on a three-strand intertwined vine that ran the full length.

Salena turned it over and over in fascination. The design was the same on both sides of the key. "It has to fit something. It was in momma's apron," said Salena.

The wheels were turning in Horatio's scheming mind. He knew that he hadn't seen anything in any of the rooms in the house that this could possibly go to...and yet, it must have been used recently or it wouldn't be in his mother's apron pocket. The shape--the cloverleaf--was jogging a foggy, faded memory of something. *What was it?*

It rushed on him all at once like a bolt of lightning. "I know where this goes, Salena!!!" he shouted so loudly that one of the carpet cleaning men turned around from his efforts on the carpet to glance at the children in the playroom. On seeing that they were being looked at, Horatio grabbed Salena's hand, pulled her into the kitchen, and spoke in hushed tones.

"Salena, this goes to a trunk in the attic. It's a really, really old one and I only got to see inside of it once a really long time ago when momma was putting away my old baby blanket and I had followed behind her when the attic stairs were down. She only let me look for a quick moment inside the trunk. I saw just the end of this key--the cloverleaf part--before she closed the trunk lid, turned it 'till it clicked really loud and then she put the key into her pocket so quickly that I didn't get a good look at the rest of it. Salena--this would be a whole lot more fun than playing dolls--let's go up in the attic and find that old trunk and see what's inside!"

"We'll get in trouble, Horatio, if momma finds out we were up there. We're not supposed to go up there without momma or daddy with us."

"Don't be such a big baby, Salena," quipped Horatio. "Momma is <u>not</u> going to find out! She's at the store and no one here is going to tell her. The carpet cleaners don't care and Matilda doesn't know we're not supposed to be up there."

Salena hesitated while turning her gaze from the ground in front of her to the ceiling above her where the attic was.

"We'll be back down before she gets home. Come on--it will be fun!"

With that assertion, Horatio the Horrible grabbed Salena the Shrieker's hand and together they headed to the hallway that lay beneath the forbidden attic.

Matilda was no longer in the hallway. The sound of the vacuum could now be heard coming from their parents' bedroom. "Great timing! Coast is clear," Horatio gleefully resounded, dragging Salena behind him. The button to lower the attic stairs was midway up the wall next to a family portrait taken last Christmas. It was a family tradition to replace it each year with the current year's photograph. Inevitably, each year's picture had at least one person looking a bit askew. This past year it had been Horatio who looked like he had sucked on a lemon before the picture was snapped.

"Darn it, Salena. It's out of my reach! Hang on. I'll get the chair from my room."

"Hurry, Horatio, before Matilda comes back!"

Salena the Shrieker didn't need to worry for in no time at all, Horatio the Horrible was back, dragging his desk chair behind him with one hand and hanging on to a flashlight with the other. He quickly positioned the chair beneath the attic stairs button, climbed on the seat, which now brought him eye level with the button. One quick push of his doughnut-sticky finger and a square panel in the ceiling above them opened. In fluid motion, the stairway descended, finishing with a soft thud on the plush maroon carpet.

"Hurry, Salena! When we get up there, there is another button that we can push and it will fold these stairs back up so no one will know where we are."

Salena did not need to be coaxed. She scampered behind Horatio, heart pounding with both fear and the excitement of what they might find up above them. As they neared the top stair step, the warm musty smell from the attic greeted their nostrils. It wasn't a bad smell, thought Salena; it made her think of the smell of old dusty newspapers and the desert after a rainstorm. As they both reached the landing, Horatio switched on his trusty flashlight so they could find their bearings in the darkness that enveloped them like the night.

"I know there is a light switch somewhere," Horatio muttered as he sent the beam of light this way and that. Salena was clinging to his shirt as she followed in step. She really did not like to be in the dark and always slept with a night light on.

"Ah, there it is!" Horatio's light beam shone on the switch on the wall to their right and a button was next to it. Horatio pushed the button first which caused the world below to close behind them with a solid thump. Then, he flipped the light switch on and the attic shapes that were frightening to Salena before now brought fascination and delight to her imaginative heart.

"Wow, look at all this stuff, Horatio! This is neat!" To Salena's six-year-old eyes, the attic did not look the dusty, chaotic mess that it was. No, to her it was a virtual treasure trove of odd shapes, sizes, colors of trunks and boxes and bags to be explored and delighted in bit by bit. She ran her fingers along an old table leaving a tell tale streak. An old baby bassinette was at the end of this table next to a box marked "Christmas decorations". Salena wanted to savor each new discovery as she peered on tippy toe here or ran there, peering beneath a cloth draped over another table. So much to explore!

Horatio was not quite as fascinated as Salena with the dusty attic treasures. He kicked at a box marked simply "Toys" and heard the rattles and jingles of what must have been his and Salena's baby things. Opening it up, he found a soft cloth ball that rattled when he shook it and he tossed it Salena's way, bouncing it off her head in the process.

"Stop it, Horatio!"

"I was just playing. Come on Salena, let's look for that trunk that fits the key."

The opening from below to the attic where the children now stood was about at midpoint of the long attic room. Only one end sported a window that had not seen a cleaning rag upon it for many a day. Faded blue ruffled curtains plus the dust encrusted window blocked out most of the outdoor lighting. There were three ceiling lights equally distanced along the long room that shed minimal light due to dust and low watt bulbs.

Salena's and Horatio's eyes had adapted to the lighting, but Horatio had left his flashlight on for exploration purposes all the same. "How about you start at that end, Salena (Horatio was pointing to the end opposite the window) and I'll start at the window end and we'll meet back here in the middle?" Salena looked down to the far end where Horatio had pointed. There were lots of dark spaces down that way that made Salena tremble inside. But, she didn't want Horatio to call her a big baby again so she quickly thought and said, "You have the flashlight, Horatio--you go to that end and I'll start here where it's lighter and go to the window."

"All right, all right. Have it your way, but let's get moving so we can find that trunk before momma gets home." And with that, he left her, noisily banging in to this and that as he made his way to the back of the attic.

Salena resisted the urge that was almost as bad as wanting the last cookie in the cookie jar to pause and open each box and bag as she moved carefully along inspecting all outward trappings only. *Somehow, I will get back up here to see what all this is,* she thought as her eyes glanced carefully about looking for a trunk that would fit that unique key tucked deep in her front jean pocket.

The problem was, there were lots of trunks littered about, but so far, they were just very ordinary looking ones and none with a key-hole that this key would fit. Some were square metal ones. Others were long, hard cardboard type--not fancy or different looking. And atop the trunks were boxes and bags of every shape and size.

Salena the Shrieker was getting a bit discouraged with all this tedious looking. She so wanted to explore and play. She did a few skips and a little leap just to liven it up a bit...and then she spied it! Several feet in front of her was a small daylight beam of light bravely making its way past the grime and grit of the curtained window, resting its glow upon the meticulously hand carved, antique trunk that had now become home to Kenny the Koala Bear.

Chapter Nine

Rick the Red-Necked Ranger rubbed his eyes that had become fixated in a blank stare at the now cold, half cup of coffee in the paper cup provided free of charge to family and friends of loved ones being tended to beyond the swinging doors of Crystal Creek's E.R. It was all such a nightmare blur to him--the horrid, sickening sound of the branch cracking beneath his precious niece Hannah's feet. That sound and the flash of horror emanating from her eyes was a sight and sound he was not sure could ever be vanquished from his brain.

He shook himself and stood up. His body had stiffened from this sitting and waiting to hear how Hannah was. The E.R. would only allow the parents, Judith and Daniel, back with Hannah and it seemed that they had been back there forever though he knew it was just the sickening trauma of adrenaline that had now drained him and settled in his empty stomach that magnified this seeming slowness of time.

Thank God for his training! Thinking back to the clearing, he remembered racing up the hill to Hannah's side after commanding the canine troops to leave in order to avoid detection. Hannah had been unconscious when he saw her and it was evident that her arm was broken by the twisted angle that it lay in. He knew that Judith and Daniel had to be at the favorite camp spot down the trail and he called on his phone to their cells after radioing for the life flight paramedics. She was breathing, but he could not tell what else might be going on inside. *Please, my dear King, let her be o.k..,* had been his brief, yet fervent prayer between calls.

At that moment, the E.R. doors swung open and a very tired and disheveled Daniel and Judith emerged. Seeing Rick caused a weak smile to come to Judith's mouth. He rushed to her in a brotherly embrace. "How is she Judith? What did the docs say?"

"They think it's just a concussion. She's been rousing in and out of consciousness. They have her arm in a cast now. She's not making much sense yet, though. She keeps mumbling about dogs having a meeting and Puss Puss B' Guss Guss in the woods. Oh, Rick, do you think she's going to be o.k.?

"Sis, we have our faith. The King of Kings has her in the palm of His hands. He has never failed those who have trusted in Him and He most certainly is not going to let this sweet one down that loves Him so much, now will He?" With those clear blue eyes of reassurance so piercingly gazing into her own, Judith had to nod in agreement.

"Daniel, what do you say to taking my sister out to eat--my treat. You both look like you need a break from here for a bit. See if we can arrange for me to go back for a bit and sit with Hannah."

Judith started a weak protest, but Daniel agreed with the Ranger. "Come on my dear--we'll be back in an hour or so. You need to eat something." Rick pressed some money into Daniel's palm and though he tried to resist, the Ranger would not allow it.

"Thank you," said Daniel. He motioned to a nurse that had just come out of the doors and introduced Rick to her. She was only too happy to usher him back.

This could be tricky, thought the Ranger as he followed in the bustling nurse's footsteps--scrambled thoughts were racing through the Ranger's mind. *I can't compromise the mission of my canines. How can I explain to dear Hannah about what she saw in the woods?* As was his custom when perplexed, he kept running his hands back and forth through his hair as though the answer would somehow come that way. But right now, his mind was as clear as deep forest mud.

Salena knelt before the trunk in excited anticipation. Even though it was very dusty, the beauty of the carved wood and the antique appearance made Salena feel that she was indeed the keeper of the key of an ancient treasure chest. She wanted to be the one to open it so she didn't call out to Horatio of her find. She hurriedly brought out the key from her pocket, inserted it into the keyhole and began turning it to the right. She heard the click, seeming quite loud in the now quiet attic, and with much excitement, she grasped the trunk lid with her small, delicate hands and slowly pushed it upward. The shock, amazement and delight of what she saw caused her to let loose a high-pitched squeal, which reached the ears of her brother and caused him to drop with a clatter an old robot toy that he had found.

"What's going on? What have you found, Salena?"

"It's the bear--the koala--momma hid him away in here!" Salena shrieked with glee as she pulled Kenny out of his nestled place on top of the quilt and hugged him to her chest, spinning round and round with him. She buried her face in his soft fur that felt so real to her cheeks. Then, lifting him up above her head, she gazed at those eyes that just seemed to look right back at her.

"You are so beautiful," she cooed.

Horatio had been crashing and tripping his way back to see what on earth Salena was making such a fuss over. When he saw her there in the dim sunlight with the bear over her head and the trunk open next to her, jealousy reared its ugly head inside of him. He ran with all his might to where she stood enraptured with her find and snatched the bear from her upward, outstretched hands.

"Nooo...Horatio--give him back, give him back!!!"

Now Horatio was holding the koala high aloft his head as he zigzagged back and forth in the narrow open space between trunks, bags and boxes.

"He's mine now--all mine!" he taunted while Salena raced after him, her small fists smacking Horatio's back whenever she got close enough for contact.

Horatio continued to run and jeer at Salena--stopping every now and again to dangle the bear in front of her just until she was within reach and then he would quickly lift him into the air and take off running again. This constant taunting and exhaustive running caused hot tears to stream down Salena's cheeks and she began her characteristic shrill wailing.

"Oh, quit it, you big baby--you're going to make Matilda come up here." And with that, he pitched the koala bear high into the air, way over Salena's head and Kenny the Koala Bear landed on top of a dresser near to the open trunk that had housed him so secretly until now.

"You're so stupid and mean, Horatio!" Salena said as she ran to rescue the bear. She climbed onto some boxes next to the dresser so she could reach him. Brushing the dust from his fur where he had landed, she again cuddled him and kissed the top of his head.

"You're just a little cry baby," Horatio said as he came over to look in the trunk where Kenny had come from. He began rummaging through its contents but nothing of interest struck him.

"This is boring anyway. I'm going back downstairs to play with my videos." He made a taunting motion at Salena like he was going to grab the bear which elicited another high pitched scream, and then darting away from her, Horatio ran to the stairway button, pushed it, and escaped the attic with a "See ya later, spoiled baby" as his head vanished down the stairs.

Calm returned to Salena the Shrieker's soul with the departure of Horatio the Horrible from the musty attic world. Salena plopped down on some old large paisley print throw pillows while still hugging Kenny the Koala Bear snugly to her small frame.

She felt such a deep sense of peace as she hugged the bear. A peace that made her feel as though she had been transported to another time and place where happiness was a constant way of life and tears and sorrow were unknown and foreign. This was a place far from cruel words, selfish brothers and screaming mothers. Salena sighed deeply with the joy of this peaceful river that seemed to cover her from head to foot.

"Wonderful, isn't it?" said Kenny the Koala Bear.

"Yes, it is," answered Salena without thinking and then startled, realizing she wasn't dreaming, dropped Kenny on the pillow, and inched backward away from him.

"Did you just talk to me?" she said quietly and very slowly.

"Yes," said Kenny the Koala Bear in his most gentle voice so as not to frighten young Salena.

"But, bears can't talk! This must be a trick or something!" Salena jumped up and began looking about just to make sure Horatio hadn't returned while she had her eyes closed hugging the bear, but no, she and the koala bear were quite alone amidst the piles of stuff in this uppermost part of the Pomposity home.

"No, this is not a trick, little one. Please don't be scared--I won't hurt you. Come back and sit down and let me talk to you."

Salena had left the bear on the pillows as she had been scurrying about to make sure that Horatio had not slipped back upstairs. Something in the way that the koala bear spoke brought a feeling of comfort to Salena that she had never felt before and that she just could not explain or even begin to understand, but yet, she felt drawn to him. She slowly walked back to the big, overstuffed pillows and sat down opposite Kenny the Koala Bear, gazing at those sparkling dark eyes that seemed to peer right through her with compassion and love.

"Where do you come from? Who are you? What's your name? Are there more bears like you? Does my momma know you can talk? Why didn't you talk the night momma brought you home? What....?"

"Slow, down, slow down, little one. One question at a time," said Kenny the Koala Bear. The King had spoken to Kenny early this morning before his release from his trunk captivity, and had well prepared him for this first meeting with Salena the Shrieker.

"Let me begin," said Kenny, "by telling you a little bit about me and about my family and then, I want to tell you about a very special King and about His Kingdom."

Thus, Kenny the Koala Bear answered Salena's questions, one by one, and began his tale about his life in the Land of the Crystal Creek folk. He told her about his momma and his happy life of scampering about the wonderful eucalyptus groves and playing in the pond with his best of friends, who was a golden retriever named Bubba Doo Wah Wah. He described the wonderful picnics they shared as well as the homemade cookies that his momma koala would bring. Salena let forth giggles of delight at hearing of the rambunctious play of Kenny and Bubba and could quite picture the happy world that Kenny had come from due to his great descriptions while the lilting tone in his voice just made it come so alive with a joy that she wished existed in her world. At the end of the story about his home life adventures, Kenny the Koala Bear paused for a moment and Salena noticed a deep reflection like a cloud moving over the sun come across his eyes that made him look a bit sad.

"Do you miss your home?" asked Salena.

"Yes, I do, but the King has me on a mission and I cannot go home until it is fulfilled."

"I thought my momma found you. What King are you talking about? And, what's a mission?"

Kenny the Koala Bear placed his paws gently on top of Salena's hands. He knew this part would be hard for such a young one to understand, but he had the King's assurance that even the very deepest things of the Kingdom could be understood by the youngest of children for all must become as a child in order to enter the Kingdom. He therefore began with confidence to share with this yearning, hungering heart the glories of the Kingdom and the majesty of the King of Kings and Lord of Lords who always reveals himself to such souls who seek Him.

Salena sat enraptured at the words of Kenny the Koala Bear. The more he talked, the happier and lighter she felt inside. "Oh, Kenny,

I want to meet your King. Can you take me to Him? I want to see this beautiful Kingdom that you've told me about!"

"One day we who choose to follow the King will indeed live in that glorious place where there is no more sorrow and everything is beautiful and glorious to behold. But the first step one must take to follow the King in order to live in that place one day is an inward step."

"An inward step?" asked Salena. "What does that mean?"

"Let me explain it this way," said Kenny the Koala Bear. "You know how when you are invited somewhere very special you take a long bubble bath to get all cleaned up so that you will smell really good and then you put on your prettiest dress and your momma fixes your hair and puts pretty ribbons in it so you will look extra special pretty?"

Salena nodded thinking about her blue taffeta lace dress that she especially liked.

"Then, you look in the mirror and you see how beautiful you look, and you feel really good?" Kenny continued.

"Yes," Salena said smiling.

"Well, keep that thought and think about the inside of you that you can't see. You can't give that part a bubble bath like your outside but deep inside of you is a part of you that has to be cleaned up and made new--and there is only one person who can do that--and that is the King!"

"How can He do that?" asked Salena.

"He does it by our believing that He is who He says He is--the King of Kings and the Lord of Lords. Then, all we have to do is ask Him to come into our hearts and He does! He cleans up everything that is dirty inside of us making us brand new inside, as sparkling as a diamond in the sunlight."

The thought of being as sparkling as Salena had seen momma Gertie's diamonds in the sunlight on the very inside of her made Salena feel quite giddy. "I want to be that sparkling right now, Kenny. What do I do?"

Kenny could already feel the King's anointed presence as he softly said to Salena: "Close your eyes and say these words after me." The words were simple yet deep and have been said for ages upon ages by all who hunger and thirst for righteousness. The simple invitation for the King of Kings and the Lord of Lords to come and live in a hungering, thirsting heart has and always will be answered.

The beam of light coming through the dusty panes of glass grew strikingly brighter as the bowed head of Salena the Shrieker said the timeless words of invitation and giving of her heart to her newfound King. As she finished speaking, she heard the Koala Bear start to sing. She opened her eyes and saw such a warmth of joy in his coal black eyes as she listened intently to his words:

> *O sing praises to the King of Kings*
> *O sing praises to the Lord of Lords*
> *For it is He who has made us*
> *And He who has saved us*
> *And He it is who loves us*
> *Now and evermore.*

Kenny the Koala Bear kept up the refrain until Salena the Shrieker caught on and soon Salena's youthful soprano voice mixed in beautiful harmony to the Koala's rich tenor tones. As they sang, they did a little hopping, marching dance about the clear attic floor space they were in--bear paws and little girl arms lifted high in the air in joyful abandon as they pranced about.

The joyful celebration dance was abruptly interrupted with Matlida's shouts echoing up the open stairway. "Salena, Salena--you up there?" Salena's joyful high turned quickly to panic as she grabbed Kenny's paw and said in a fervent hushed tone: "What do I do now?"

"Not to panic, little one," soothed Kenny the Koala Bear and with a hop, skip and a jump he was back in the antique trunk.

"Will you be o.k. in there?" said Salena.

"I will be fine. The King of Kings takes care of me."

75

"I'll come back as quick as I can," promised Salena.

"I know you will," smiled Kenny. "Don't forget our song. Sing it often. He likes the praises of His children!"

"I will," promised Salena as she hurriedly closed the trunk lid, turned the key 'til the loud click rang out, and then pocketed the key in her deep jean pocket.

"Coming, Matilda, I'm coming," she said scurrying to the light, and flipping the switch to turn it off.

Kenny could hear the small feet scampering away to go down the stairs and then the whir of the staircase closing back into the attic space. Silence and darkness returned to the upper-room world and to the confines of Kenny the Koala Bear's trunk home, but Kenny's heart knew no bounds as the joy and peace of the King flooded his being. The deep, familiar voice spoke within him in warm, approving tones: *"Your mission has begun."*

Katie Koala paused in her kitchen brushing the remaining flour off her faded gingham print apron collected there from an afternoon of bread baking. She gazed out the kitchen window with the view of the late afternoon's golds and reds from the sun soon to set playing a colorful palette over the deep blue-green pond. Something was different in this moment. She sensed it deep within her soul. Even though no new news had come her way from the Corps regarding her beloved son Kenny the Koala Bear's whereabouts, she felt that right at this very moment something special had happened that Kenny was a very important part of. She could not explain it with her logical mind, but she just knew it was so. She knelt down and gave the King thanks for reassuring her mother's tender heart that still yearned to see her sweet bear's face but this special assurance growing within her gave her grace to be patient. "Give him a hug for me, my King and keep him safe," she said aloud. And she knew He would.

Chapter Ten

The abrupt dismissal of the canine troops by Rick the Red-Necked Ranger had sent Puss Puss B' Guss Guss into a feline frenzy. Not only had Bubba Doo Wah Wah's rearing up on his hind legs landed Puss Puss B' Guss Guss square on his backside in the red dusty earth beneath Bubba's hindquarters, but now, noisy drooling canines were everywhere stirring up even more of the earth and sending all of its tiny red particles to cling all over the fastidious feline's white coat. Puss Puss B' Guss Guss was already in a tizzy over seeing his owner Hannah fall out of that tree and would have headed straight up the hill along with Rick the Red-Necked Ranger if Bubba Doo Wah Wah had not reached down and grabbed him with his jowls.

"Let me go, you mangy dog," he hissed at Bubba.

"Cool your jets, Puss Puss. We can't go up there. You cannot give us away by letting your owner see you," he said while sidestepping away from the fray of dogs racing to leave the woods.

And with that statement, he tossed the Puss Puss up over his head in order for him to land on his back so he could get into the backpack. Puss Puss B' Guss Guss landed with a *meowr* and a hiss.

"You love doing that, don't you?"

"Yep, you are a fun cat-a-pult," teased Bubba.

"Ha, ha, dog bone breath," said Puss Puss nosing his way deep in the backpack and turning around several times, he finally settled in his typical feline curl.

"Onward, for the Corps!" bellowed Bubba and off he went at galloping speed through the autumn leafed trails of Pine Valley Forest. The rocking rhythm of the large dog's gait soon soothed the temperament of the frazzled feline, and he relaxed into peaceable kitty slumber as Bubba Doo Wah Wah headed to the homeward haven that was Crystal Creek.

Rick stood hesitantly in the doorway gazing at the pale shade of his niece's face that was such a stark contrast to her normal rosy-cheeked glow that was so familiar to him. Her frame seemed so small in the sterile white linen, steel-sided hospital bed. The nurse had already entered the room and motioned him in. The Ranger, usually so full of courage and a take charge attitude, felt so small and weak inside as he neared Hannah's side.

"She probably won't wake up for awhile. We gave her a sedative to help her sleep. She was getting a bit agitated when her folks were here and at this point, she just needs to rest and re-coup a bit from all this recent trauma her system has gone through with the fall and having her arm set."

"How long will she be here?" the Ranger managed to choke out in halting tones.

"Oh, more than likely, no more than a few days just to make sure she's stable enough to go home." Seeing the sadness in the Ranger's eyes, the nurse put forth a reassuring hand on his shoulder. "She's going to be just fine. She just needs some TLC. Here, sit in this chair so you can be close to her. I'll be right down the hall if you need anything." With a comforting smile and a pat on the Ranger's back, the nurse hurried from the room to tend to her other patients.

Rick slowly settled into the chair provided for him next to Hannah's bed. He gazed at the sleeping girl with deep affection in his heart. "She's so precious, my King," he said quietly. Laying his work worn, calloused hand gently on her forehead, he prayed: "Let your healing virtue flow into this, your servant. Please let her be made whole again, my Lord." Hannah stirred a bit at the Ranger's prayer and she half-way opened her eyes, but then sleepily closed them before she could focus on the look of concern in the deep blue eyes of the Ranger that were so intently directed at her. The Ranger felt the powerful yet comforting presence of the King as he prayed and his large frame visibly relaxed as the deep inner realization flowed through his being that his niece truly would be all right. With an affectionate stroke to the blond tussled hair on the pillow, the Ranger withdrew his hand and lifted it upward in a "thank you" gesture before leaning back in the chair to rest in the first calm he had felt for many hours. Soon two bodies were at rest: one sporting little girl snores barely audible in the confines of the hospital room and the second with something akin to a saw blade running amuck, echoing loudly down the hallway of this small town hospital.

Bubba Doo Wah Wah rounded the last corner turn into Puss Puss B' Guss Guss' neighborhood with a slowing gait in order to assess who might be out and about. He was quite wearied from this over 24-hour adventure and every part of him ached. His stomach was growling as well, and all he wanted at this point was a good bowl of chow and eight hours shut eye. But right now, he had to keep his weary mind intent and alert in order to get this pesky feline back into his home without alerting attention to himself in the process. As it was now mid-day, he didn't have the luxury of the cover of darkness as before and every movement as he approached Puss Puss' entrance to the home must be executed with great caution.

A few folks were out and about in the neighborhood as well as a bit of car traffic. Bubba Doo Wah Wah rapidly raced for the bushes across the street after a car and bicycle went by in front of the targeted home. "Wake up, Puss Puss," he growled as he dove for cover in the bushes just in time to avoid being spotted by a mom pushing her young toddler in a stroller on the sidewalk.

"We there yet?" meowed the feline with a sleepy lack of enthusiasm.

"Yes, fur ball, we're almost to the entrance," Bubba gruffly replied. "When I say go, you need to be up and Adam and off of my back--both literally and figuratively!"

"My, aren't we in a mood--and they say that we cats are temperamental!" quipped the Puss Puss.

"Listen, you bag of fleas--it's been a long night and I am not in the mood to be spotted because of an inept exit on your part and spending a night in the dog pound!"

"Calm down, drool dog--I've got this!"

"And remember," said Bubba, "we will be expecting a report from you and your fellow fish lovers by week's end. I will come back of an evening to find out what you've learned."

"Don't sweat it. We felines are good. We'll have info on Kenny's whereabouts before you and your tick carrier buddies can say dog biscuit!"

At that insult to his canine breed and the Corps, Bubba bristled. "We'll see about that, fluffy drawers!"

Throughout all the playful bantering, Bubba stealthily inched his way through the bushes, carefully positioning himself next to the planter in front of the window.

"Do your meow thing, fish breath."

"Will do--see you soon, baggy bones." With a shrill *meowr* the Puss Puss exited the backpack and the little barrel door swung open at the base of the planter. The large fluffy fur ball that was Puss Puss B' Guss Guss entered its inner sanctum, scampering into the tunnel that led upwards to the inside of the kitty tree. He then deftly popped open the spring-loaded door, exiting at the very top of its blue carpeted ledge. He gave a little hop out of the tunnel and the carpet closed back into place hiding its hinged edge in the lush carpet. Perched at the highest point of the kitty tree and turning his head towards the window, Puss Puss caught the rear tail view of Bubba Doo Wah Wah loping down the road with nary a glance backward. Even though Puss Puss B' Guss Guss would never admit it to Bubba's face, he secretly respected the dog as once upon a time, that drool jowl had been responsible for saving Puss Puss' very life. But now was not the time for reminiscing. It definitely <u>was</u> the time for more urgent pursuits. Like attending to his rumbling stomach. With a great kitty sigh of relief at being back in his beloved home once again, Puss Puss deftly jumped down from the tree to where his beloved food dish awaited and crunched the tasty morsels like there was no tomorrow. Puss Puss B' Guss Guss was indeed safe and content once again in his cat kingdom domain with none the wiser.

Matilda was poised at the bottom of the attic stairs, hands on hips and a perplexed look on her face as Salena scrambled down the stairs as fast as she could. "Watcha doin' up there? Momma be mad if knew, momma be mad," Matilda scolded in her broken English.

"No, Matilda, it's o.k. Really," reassured Salena. "I didn't hurt anything up there--just playing." Salena threw her arms around Matilda's waist. "Please don't say anything Matilda. I didn't do anything bad up there--please?"

"You sure no make mess there?"

"Yes, Matilda, I'm sure. Just looked around, played and had fun. Nothing for momma to be upset about."

"O.k., little girl. You win. No tell momma. Be good now. Play playroom."

"Thank you, Matilda." And with one more quick hug, Salena skipped down the hall to the playroom. She felt such a joy and light-heartedness inside of her that she just did not know how to explain. Was this the new life that Kenny had told her about? She thought about the song he had taught her and she felt it bubbling forth within her now. So much so that while she was setting her dolls up around her little play table, she just had to let it come forth out of her mouth:

O sing praises to the King of Kings
O sing praises to the Lord of Lords
For it is He who has made us
And He who has saved us
And He it is who loves us
Now and evermore.

Salena kept singing this happy refrain over and over again while she brushed her dolls' hair, fussed with their clothes, and pretended to pour them tea. (No more real tea was allowed since the living room debacle). So enraptured was she with this new song she had learned that she didn't even notice the clatter of mother Gertie's high heels on the kitchen tile as she came near to Salena. The joy just seemed to envelop her as a cloud and the more she sang, the more joy she felt and the more oblivious she became to everything around her.

"Salena, Salena! What on earth is that nonsense you are singing?"

Startled abruptly back to her present surroundings by her mother's angry tone, Salena looked up into the scowling face of momma Gertie. That familiar daunting look that often frightened Salena could not even phase the joy in Salena's heart now.

"Oh, momma, it's the most wonderful song--the best song--my friend Kenny taught it to me--I can teach you too, momma!" Salena was fairly exploding. Words were tumbling out from her before her mind could even catch up to what she had just said.

"Your friend, Kenny? Who is Kenny? Did you have someone over while I was gone?"

"No, momma. No one came over. Kenny is my...is my...is my..." Salena stammered wondering really how to explain all of this.

"Kenny is your, what?" Greedy Gertie had never been known for her patience and something about that song really irritated her. She wanted to get to the bottom of this and was growing exasperated. "Kenny is your, what?!" she said much louder.

"Kenny is my... bear friend," said Salena softly.

"Oh, for heaven's sake--a stuffed play friend. Well, whatever. Just sing something else. And more quietly," she added. "I have a headache from the shopping. Looks like the carpet cleaners are about done. Probably Matilda as well. Let me take care of them. There's some cookies on the counter if you want a snack--but eat it in there, please." And off she went before Salena could explain any further.

Did momma really say she didn't like the song? How could that be? And why is she always so angry? For the first time in her tender life, Salena felt a bit sad for her mother. But she really could not explain why.

Chapter Eleven

*S*he was falling. Dogs barking. And Puss Puss' loud meow. Sharp pain. Then nothing. Then a foggy sensation of someone picking her up. Loud whirring. Going up very fast. But not awake. A dream? Muffled voices. Then ear piercing sirens. So dark. It hurts so bad--she wanted to yell out--but couldn't--eyes won't open...

"Hannah, Hannah. Wake up. Breakfast awaits, princess girl." Groggily, through heavy lidded, barely open eyes, Hannah saw a colorful, animal printed, uniformed-nurse-type person, holding a tray and then fastening it onto the tray table in front of her.

"Well, it's not the Ritz, but, the food isn't too bad around here. Sausage and pancakes this morning, I see," said the nurse as she lifted the cover to reveal the plate's contents. "And a fruit chaser. Together with your favorite, I understand, chocolate milk to wash it all down with."

"Where's my mom and dad?"

"Should be by later this morning. They were both here half the night 'til we chased them home to get some rest. Your Uncle Rick was here before that."

"Uncle Rick? I don't remember seeing him. When was he here?"

"You were out of it when he came by--stayed for a few hours though. Boy, can that man snore! Quite entertaining for the nurses' station outside your room. Anyway, little girl, let's get started on that breakfast before it gets cold. Need you to get strong so you can leave this fun-filled place soon, ya know?" The nurse plopped the chart noisily back into the holder at the end of Hannah's bed and after shooting a parting smile in Hannah's direction, she was gone. Hannah was left to her groggy, still confused thoughts as she paused to give thanks to her King for the breakfast fare.

Picking up her knife and fork, she realized that she actually was quite famished. Everything was a dream-like blur since the fall in the woods and the last meal she remembered enjoying was the cookout with her parents on their first night in the woods.

Hannah poured some more warm maple syrup over the pancakes, which flowed into little pools under the sausage links on the plate. Hungrily, she devoured them barely relishing their taste. She was just finishing her last bite of the fruit cocktail and down to one last swallow of chocolate milk when Doc Greenwood walked in.

"Well, my, my, my, if it isn't Hannah Banana in person!"

Doc Greenwood had been Hannah's doctor since she was an infant. He had always lovingly and affectionately termed her Hannah Banana. Though he was getting a bit up in years, brown hair now turned a silver grey, he still possessed a boyish twinkle in his blue eyes. Hannah hadn't seen him in quite awhile since he had moved his practice to a more rural area surrounding Crystal Creek, but she was delighted to see this familiar face from the past.

"How's the green forest, these days," Hannah quipped back, playfully teasing him about his name.

"Good to see you still have your sweet wit and sense of humor considering your latest tree escapades. Whatever possessed a smart tree climber like you to go out on such a thin limb?"

"How do you know about that, doc?"

"Oh, I have my ways," he said with a teasing grin. "Actually, since my move to the rural clinic, I am not too far from your Uncle Rick's Ranger station and he keeps me up to date on you and the family. He actually radioed me the day you fell after contacting the Life Flight folks that came on the double to rescue you out of the forest. I met up with the ambulance when you got to the ER, but you were in and out of this mundane world--probably too busy dreaming up your next adventure, no doubt?"

Doc Greenwood always had the knack of using humor to provide calm, lightness and ease to even the most desperate of situations--a trait Hannah always loved.

"I can't remember much after my fall--but, I am sure I saw Uncle Rick talking to a pack of dogs in the woods before I did--and I could swear that one of them had my Puss Puss B' Guss Guss in a backpack on his back!"

Doc Greenwood raised a bushy eyebrow in an expression of both amusement and questioning as he pulled the stethoscope out of his lab coat and placed it around his neck. "Well, Hannah Banana, you as well as your wild but endearingly creative imagination are just the same as ever. Let's have a listen, shall we? Deep breath now."

And with that, Hannah was silenced for the moment as Doc Greenwood listened to her breathing via the stethoscope placed upon her back. After several breaths, he said, "Sounds good. Now let's check out those eyes. That's got to be where the problem is for not seeing the difference between a wide branch (at this point he held his arms as far apart as he could) and a teensy, tiny one." (He motioned with one hand now, thumb and forefinger a half inch apart.) The doc's antics elicited an infectious giggle from Hannah the patient as he used the light scope to peer closely into each eye.

"Nope. They look fine. Let's see if it's the brain messing things up. Follow my finger with your eyes." Hannah almost couldn't do so as she couldn't quit giggling.

"Nope. That's not the problem. Hmmm....what could it be? Let me look in my notebook here." The doc produced a spiral from his shirt coat pocket and leafed through it with great drama and rustling of pages. "Ahhh, hahh--here it is! I knew I could solve this case."

"You have...a severe case of adventure-itis. The recommended cure is to obey your parents by not venturing off on trails without them in the future. Thus, you will avoid personal injury to your precious, precocious being," he said with manufactured, stern vehemence betrayed by a tell-tale twinkle in his eye. "Your doctor-ordered recovery plan is to go home with said parents this afternoon and look so pitiful that they forget to lecture you, since I already have. My plan should have the delightful result of getting you a big bowl of ice cream. This doctor further gives you strict orders to rest in bed for the next couple of days. What do you say to that, Miss Hannah Banana?"

"Sounds good to me. I want to get home to my own room and to cuddle with Puss Puss B' Guss Guss. Bet he misses me!"

"I bet so, little one. Well, I'm writing your diagnosis in this chart together with some home care instructions that I'll give to your nurse to go over with you and I'll make sure that your parents know that I've been by and have got you firmly back on the right track!" He gave Hannah's shoulder a pat and then pointed his finger at her, trying again to look stern, but Hannah wasn't fooled.

"Be good now or those dogs in the woods might come find you!"

Hannah responded with a giggle, the doc gave a wave, and off he went onto his rounds.

Hannah pushed her tray table away and pressed the remote button to the TV. A program was on where show dogs competed in an indoor arena. Hannah's thoughts flooded back to the woods and the pack of what seemed like a hundred dogs--*was it my imagination? Or was it real?* Right at this moment, she just wasn't sure. As she watched the dogs perform their antics on the television, she decided not to worry about it. *Getting back home this afternoon will help me sort it out. My mind is just too cloudy to figure it out right now.* Hannah leaned her head back on the pillow in peace at her new resolve. The performing dogs in the ring and the barking dogs in the woods were sleepily blending into one scenario.

Pugnacious Pomposity, III returned home from work that Saturday evening to a home as well ordered and ticking in sync as a Swiss watch. The home smelled of lemon oil from Matilda's meticulous furniture dusting plus the tantalizing garlic and rosemary fragrances wafting from the kitchen where the dinner chicken was roasting in the oven. As Mr. Pomposity came down the hallway from the garage entrance, he glanced towards the living room, its plush carpet restored once more to pristine white glistening strands with no trace of the rancid oily spots or ugly brown tea stains from the ruckus of yesterday. *This is the way my home should be,* he mused, *order, discipline, and myself as king of my domain.*

He paused in his inward ego musings as the sound of singing reached his ears. This was odd indeed. Usually he was greeted by the ear piercing screams of Salena generally due to young Horatio's torments. He wondered if perhaps the family was out back and had left a radio on as no one had rushed to greet him as usual. As he came around the corner, he saw a sight that both shocked and startled him. There was his young daughter, eyes closed, hands upraised, swaying slightly and singing with all her might:

> *O sing praises to the King of Kings*
> *O sing praises to the Lord of Lords*
> *For it is He who has made us*
> *And He who has saved us*
> *And He it is who loves us*
> *Now and evermore.*

As Pugnacious Pomposity, III stood there, halted in his tracks from his usual brisk gait, staring at his singing daughter, he realized that he had never ever heard his daughter sing anything before--not a nursery rhyme, not a jingle from a television commercial, nothing at all that he could remember. She was either speaking or shrieking, but <u>never</u> singing! So--where on earth did this song about some king come from?

Salena, sensing that she was no longer by herself in the playroom, opened her eyes to see the puzzled face of her father looking down at her. "Oh, daddy, daddy, I have had the most wonderful day!" she exclaimed with arms now outstretched towards Pugnacious Pomposity, III for him to pick her up, which he readily obliged her.

88

"Indeed, child--did it involve singing lessons? I have never heard that song before. In fact, I have never heard you sing. Who came over today to teach you?"

"Kenny did, daddy--he's so wonderful!"

"Kenny--who on earth is Kenny?"

Before Salena had a chance to explain about Kenny the Koala Bear, the back door banged open, rattling the venetian blinds as it hit the doorstop. Horatio the Horrible burst into the room holding a mason jar in his dusty, grimy hands, with a big mischievous grin on his face.

"Look what I caught!" he exclaimed with pride holding the jar up for Pugnacious Pomposity, III to see.

"Oh, my, that looks like a *phrynosoma solare.*"

"What's that, daddy?" Salena asked straining on tippy toe to peer at the jar above her head.

Pugnacious Pomposity, III lowered the jar for Salena to look at as he had taken it out of Horatio's hands for a better look himself. "You children would know this by its more common name. It's a desert horned toad."

"He's kind of cute," said Salena looking at the small tan as desert sand toad now at her eye level.

"He's not cute!" shouted Horatio, grabbing the jar abruptly out of his father's hands. "He's a warrior toad and he's going to live in my room and grow up to be as big as a dragon." And with that exclamation, Horatio the Horrible began running from the playroom down the hall. "And when he becomes a dragon, he's going to eat you, Salena!" he yelled before the slamming door to his room acted as a final forceful punctuation mark to his rude words.

Pugnacious braced himself for the inevitable high-pitched wailing, which always proceeded from Salena following these daily taunts from her brother. But, to his utter amazement, Salena looked up at him, gave a smile, and turned with a little hop and a skip and pranced over to where her dolls were seated around her tea table. As he stared at her in complete bewilderment, she began humming as she pretended to pour tea for her dolls.

"Are you feeling o.k., Salena?"

"Never better, daddy!"

Not able to make his logical mind wrap around this strange behavior any longer, Pugnacious Pomposity, III left his happily humming daughter in search of Greedy Gertie. *Something very strange has taken place in my home today and I am determined to get to the bottom of this,* were the thoughts screaming through his perplexed mind. "Gertie, where are you....Gertie?!"

Chapter Twelve

Judith and Daniel Stillwaters were delighted when they heard the news upon arriving at the hospital that sunny Sunday afternoon that Doc Greenwood had given his medical o.k. to release Hannah to home care. To their great relief, it turned out that Hannah did not have a concussion as previously thought and all tests showed that she would not have to stay at the hospital any longer--just home care and a check up in 4 weeks to see if her arm had healed enough for the cast to be removed.

After the nurse reviewed the doc's home care instructions, including, to the dismay of Hannah, the admonitions for strict bed rest for the next two days, graduating to return to light activity later in the week, Hannah was helped into a wheelchair and whisked to the hospital's entrance where Daniel had brought the car around, ready and warm for their precious one's ride home. Judith climbed in the back in true mother fashion to let Hannah rest her head upon her for the journey home. Hannah didn't mind the extra motherly fussing as she still felt groggy and tired, but very happy that she would soon be in her own bed cuddling Puss Puss B' Guss Guss' warm, furry body close to her. She imagined his rumbling purrs on the drive home, but, every time she closed her eyes, the disturbing scene of the barking dogs in the woods haunted her. Still, she wondered how much was real and how much might have been affected in her memory from the jar of the fall.

Momma was saying something that her deep thoughts had shut out. "What's that, momma?"

"I was just saying that when we get home, I want you to change into your comfy p.j.'s, and I'll fix you a nice snack to tide you over until dinner."

"Sounds good, momma," Hanna replied as she nestled her head against momma's chest again and relaxed under her momma's gentle stroking of her hair.

The ride went quickly and soon they were pulling into the driveway of their familiar homestead. "Put your arms around my neck, little pumpkin girl, and I'll carry you in," said Daniel Stillwaters as he opened the back seat car door. He knelt down so Hannah could reach his neck and in one strong fatherly swoop, Hannah was securely in his arms. Judith slipped out the other side, reaching the front door before they arrived in order to open it wide for father and daughter to pass through with ease. Once they were safely over the threshold, Daniel gently set his daughter down in the foyer. Judith was already in the kitchen, in true mother fashion, intent on caring for her wounded cub. "How does pizza bites sound for a snack?" came her lilting voice from the kitchen.

"Great, momma. Can I have some chocolate milk with that?"

"Sure thing," answered momma followed by: "Get your jammies on now while this is cooking." Hannah was already heading for her bedroom in search of Puss Puss B' Guss Guss as the last direction from momma reached her ears. She didn't have far to look upon entering her warm cozy bedroom. There lay her regal feline stretched out in the late afternoon sun atop his beloved kitty tree.

"Oh, Puss Puss, I am so glad to be home!" Hannah rushed for her fluffy kitty and buried her face in his soft belly of white silk. She stroked his head and skritched behind his ears. Soon the familiar rumbling purrs enveloped her and kitty and owner rested in contentment.

"Hannah," dad said peering around the door, "don't forget to get your p.j.'s on--your snack should be ready soon."

"O.k., dad." Sighing, Hannah relinquished her stroking of the purring Puss Puss to deal with the changing of clothes.

"Do you need mom's help? I know it must be awkward with that cast."

"No, dad, I'll be fine. But, I do need another hug first."

"That, I can do." Hannah loved her father's hugs and always felt safe in his strong arms that made her feel like she was hugging a large teddy bear.

"O.k., pumpkin girl--get changed now." And dad Daniel left the room, quietly closing her door behind him.

Hannah quickly found her favorite p.j.'s in the second drawer of her old oak dresser. They had been a present from last Christmas--blue fleece with white kitty cats frolicking about in a random pattern throughout the material. They made her think of Puss Puss B' Guss Guss as a kitten--always bounding about chasing this and that--the "mighty hunter" kitty. It was a bit more difficult maneuvering her clothes due to the cast, but the pajama top was loose and big, easily fitting over her cast.

As soon as she was dressed, she went back to her beloved Puss Puss--rubbing every inch of his fur. He started playfully batting at her as she tickled his paws, which always made Hannah giggle. He never hurt her with his claws, as he was a gentle sort. As she batted him back, her finger touched something on one of his back hind paws that felt sticky. "What's this, Puss Puss?" Hannah stopped batting at him and gently stroked him to calm him as she took his left hind paw in her hands. There it was--small, but definite. An almost unnoticeable round spot. Dark. Sticky. Leaning over, she sniffed it. A smell she was quite familiar with from many camp outs reached her nostrils. No mistaking this scent. Definitely pine sap! While this shocking revelation rolled about in her mind, her gaze turned from Puss Puss B' Guss Guss to the view out the window behind him. The sun streaming in the window outlined the next jarring bit of evidence: two large, muddy dog paw prints on the window!

Hannah turned with a start and burst from her room, almost tripping in her haste. "Mom, dad, come quick! I have proof that Puss Puss was in the woods! It wasn't a dream--it wasn't a dream!!!"

Pugnacious Pomposity, III found Greedy Gertie primping in front of their large vanity mirror that hung above the dark, cherry wood dresser imported from the Orient. She was seated on the delicately brocaded chair in such a fashion as to make one think they had intruded upon a queen busily attending to her beauty regimen. Her reflection in the mirror was one of a disdaining glare meant solely for him as she brushed her coal black hair with her pearl handled brush.

"Really, Pugnacious, why are you hollering for me so? You sound like our whiny children! Dinner is almost ready. What do you need?!"

Pugnacious Pomposity, III would never allow anyone to speak to him in the rude fashion that was his wife's way without giving them a tongue lashing that would reduce the other party to a pile of shreds cowering at his feet. In truth, he secretly feared Greedy Gertie, as she had quite a vengeful streak that he had learned not to engage if he wanted peace in his home.

"I am sorry, my darling Gertie," he soothed while placing his hands in comforting fashion upon her bony shoulders. "It's simply that I have just witnessed the most distressing event in the playroom only moments ago."

"Distressing? Whatever do you mean, Pugnacious?" said Gertie while rising to look for her earrings as the rest of her ensemble, make-up and evening dress clothes, was now complete. Saturday evening was generally a date night--sometimes for dinner and a movie--other times, a home meal with the children and then out for dancing or visiting with friends until the wee hours of the morning.

"I don't know how to explain it exactly, my dear. It was just so very strange," said Pugnacious Pomposity, III as he adjusted his tie while gazing in the mirror. Turning towards Greedy Gertie who had now found her favorite diamond dangly earrings, he said with great drama in a hushed voice, "She, our daughter, Salena, was......singing!"

"Oh, for heaven's sakes, Pugnacious, I thought something truly awful had just happened." Greedy Gertie was now positioned back in front of the mirror admiring the way the light glittered and sparkled in such radiance off of her long diamond earrings as well as the large diamond necklace that hung around her bony neck.

"It's probably that stupidly irritating song she was singing earlier when I got home--some ridiculous song about a king."

"Yes...that's it! It was like she was mesmerized, in a trance, I might add, with both her hands lifted up and eyes closed and swaying like this," as Pugnacious Pomposity, III was explaining to Greedy Gertie what he had seen, he began demonstrating the same for Gertie's viewing.

"Oh, stop that Pugnacious. Put your hands down. You look like an idiot!"

"But, Gertie--listen to me! Salena said that someone named Kenny taught her this song. Salena has never ever sung before. Who is Kenny and why was I not informed that our daughter was to be receiving private singing instruction without my approval?" Gertie was now practically bent over, with her disturbing, cackling laughter filling the bedroom.

When she finally regained her composure enough to speak, she spewed out with great delight at being one up on her husband: "Kenny is a bear--a stuffed bear! Some silly old toy in Salena's room. Probably a present we gave her a long time ago, you know, an imaginary play friend! Oh, really, Pugnacious, sometimes you are the most foolish man I know!"

Gertie swirled around admiring the flow of her long evening gown. "Time for dinner, my silly husband, " Gertie admonished while leaving the bedroom, "and then off for a night of dancing," she said in shrill falsetto from the hallway.

"But, Gertie...Gertie...Gertie?!" No answer was returned to his calls.   Pugnacious Pomposity, III, like a balloon that had suddenly deflated, sat down on the edge of the bed, and aloud, and only to himself and the bedroom walls surrounding him said: "This was much too real and precious to have come from something imaginary."

Chapter Thirteen

"*Whooo......Whooo......Whooo......Whooo......*" The gentle owl song alarm clock that had been a gift from Hannah to her favorite Uncle Rick the Red-Necked Ranger, was demanding his attention at its 5:00 A.M. wake-up call. The sleepy ranger clumsily shut it off, knocking over an empty metal coffee cup that clattered noisily to the floor of his bedroom/living room in the lookout tower. The sound jarred him awake and he reluctantly sat up in bed, rubbing his hair back and forth with his hands in characteristic ranger fashion. The enticing smell of coffee brewing came from his little kitchenette as it was set for 5:00 A.M. as well on automatic timer. Swinging his legs over the bed, he found his well worn, but cozy warm slippers and slipped into them while grabbing his flannel robe from the foot post of his hand-carved bed. Heading for the very tiny half-bathroom that just had space in it for a sink, toilet and narrow shower, he splashed some water on his face to complete his wake-up process.

Returning to the main room where his bed was, Rick retrieved the blue metal coffee cup from under the end table where it had rolled when he knocked it off. He absentmindedly rinsed it in the sink and poured the now ready, steaming black coffee into it. In auto pilot mode, he added powdered creamer and sugar, stirred it while checking the countertop to see if there were any doughnuts left in the box from yesterday. *Ahh, yes!* One lone chocolate cake doughnut remained. Grasping his find in one hand while balancing his coffee cup in the other, he shuffled back to the main room and settled himself in his favorite overstuffed, worn brown leather recliner that faced the east and the view of the woods that was truly spectacular when the first rays of sunrise revealed their verdant green. Now that fall was here, the evergreen pines were mixed with trees that changed colors and the beauty of this season with the crimson, gold, orange and green of the Pine Valley Forest was one that Rick the Red-Necked Ranger truly enjoyed.

But this season had brought trouble. With Kenny the Koala Bear missing and his concerns for the recovery of his favorite niece Hannah, the Ranger's mind was restless and uneasiness had replaced his general jovial relaxed nature. Since last Saturday and the visit to the hospital, the week had flown quickly by as he had returned to the forest late that same day. Now it was already a week later, and he was expecting a meeting at 8:00 A.M. this morning with Sergeant Bubba Doo Wah Wah, Lance Corporal James the beagle and Corporal Gerald, the German shepherd. He was hopeful that he would at least have a lead from his top three dogs on the case-- something to ease Katie the Koala Bear's motherly mind and heart. The rural forces had been engaged since last Sunday when he met with General Johnson of the Koala Bear unit of the Corps and the koala bears still had nary a clue even though they had scoured a large region of the surrounding Crystal Creek countryside. Perhaps the feline forces with Puss Puss B' Guss Guss as lead cat might have found something to go on. Rick knew that Bubba would know if this was the case, and he was hopeful of a good report at this morning's meeting.

Rick took another bite of his doughnut and washed it down with a hot mouthful of coffee. A few rays of light were beginning to show by the tree line. *Time to greet the morning properly,* he thought remembering that in spite of this truly disturbing week, he was not alone. One more powerful than he had all of this under control. Finishing his coffee and last morsel of doughnut, the rough and tough Ranger bowed his head and silently gave all his troubles, as well as all of his praises of thanksgiving to his King: the King of Kings and Lord of Lords!

Try as she might, Salena just couldn't tie the blue ribbon atop her head. She was so excited for today to arrive that she had set her clothes out the night before in anticipation. Her favorite Fanny the Fairy Princess sneakers with pink sparkling stars on a white leather background now shod her feet beneath her designer denim Country Girl jeans and her special t-shirt given her by her father last birthday that said "Daddy's Little Princess" in blue sparkly lettering. She had just brushed her long dark hair and wanted to tie it back with her ribbon in a bow for flair, but bows were still a mystery. All her sneakers were Velcro and she just could not figure the bow concept out yet.

"Momma, momma! I need help with my bow!" she hollered as she heard mother Gertie coming down the hall.

"I'm trying to get your brother moving, Salena--hang on! I'll be there in a minute."

This was the reason Salena was so excited. Momma and Horatio would soon be leaving the house and she had talked momma into leaving her home with Matilda while momma took Horatio to his first clarinet lesson this Saturday morning. Last Saturday evening at dinner Pugnacious Pomposity, III had announced to the family that he had decided that Horatio was in need of an outlet for all his "wasted energy" as he put it, and that the discipline and time required for learning a musical instrument was just the ticket to help Horatio to direct his energy into more "positive pursuits".

Salena didn't care about all the big words her father used that night or whether Horatio learned to play anything at all. She was simply and thoroughly excited that this would give her the exact opportunity she needed to get back up to the attic to talk with her beloved Kenny the Koala Bear and learn more about the King of Kings. Since last Saturday, she had been counting down the days and she had felt that she would fairly burst open if this day had not arrived as quickly as it had. She had been fervently singing the song Kenny had taught her all week long though not in momma's presence because it seemed to irritate her so. She hoped Kenny would teach her more songs to sing to her King today and perhaps tell her more about the Kingdom that belonged to Him and sounded so beautiful!

Momma Gertie appeared in the doorway of her room together with a well-groomed Horatio. As they came in the room, Salena could not help but giggle as she looked at her brother who was visibly uncomfortable in his white starched dress shirt, dark blue tie and dark blue dress trousers and highly polished black leather shoes. His hair that most of the time stuck up this way and that was slicked down with some type of gel.

"What are you laughing about, pig face?" Horatio the Horrible said as nastily as he could in response to Salena and her giggles.

"Horatio, keep your mouth shut. Salena, quit laughing and hold still now. Let me get this bow tied."

Gertie deftly made a big bow atop Salena's head, which made Salena smile as big as sunshine when she looked at herself in her dresser mirror.

"Thank you, momma!" she said and in her joy to leave her room to go get the Saturday morning doughnuts that were always there as a weekend treat, she didn't notice that Horatio had stuck his foot out so that she would trip. Crashing to the floor, she bumped her head on the foot of the dresser.

Horatio howled with laughter at his mean trick on his sister. Ever since the day in the attic, he felt his hatred of her growing stronger in a way that he just couldn't explain.

"Horatio, you cruel brat! If it weren't for your father's strict orders that we go to this clarinet lesson this morning, I would send you to your room for the rest of the day with no food or water 'til tomorrow," said Greedy Gertie while grabbing a hold of Horatio the Horrible's ear and pulling him to the doorway.

"Go get in the car right now and wait for me--and don't touch anything in the car or you won't sit down for a week--do you understand me?!" And for emphasis, Gertie gave him a sound whack on his backside to send him whimpering on his way.

Gertie then got down on her knees on the carpet where Salena laid huddled and stroked her hair. "Are you o.k. my little princess? Come on now and get up and we'll get some ice for you. Did you bump your head or cheek?" she asked gently as she helped Salena up.

Salena's giggles had turned to sobs as her head hurt from the fall. She didn't feel like shrieking though as she normally would have in the past before Kenny had introduced her to the King. "My head, momma--back here," Salena pointed to the crown of her head. Her pretty blue ribbon was now quite askew, and leaning to the side.

"We'll get some ice on it right away," momma Gertie assured her as they walked down the hallway to the kitchen. Gertie got a small plastic zip type baggy from the pantry and grabbed a few ice cubes from the freezer to place inside it. She placed it on top of Salena's head and said, "Now, hold it here for a moment and I'll get you your milk. Your doughnut is already on the plate there."

Salena sat down on the kitchen stool that easily fit under the counter. With one hand on the ice bag, the other picked up her comfort food: the pink iced doughnut.

"There you go, sweet girl," said momma as she set the milk cup down. "Keep that ice on your head as much as possible. It will help to keep a bump from forming. Does it hurt bad still?"

"Not so much now, momma. I'll be o.k. Don't worry. I love you, momma!"

Greedy Gertie stopped stone still at these last unexpected words, feeling a tug at her heart that she could not explain. *Had her daughter ever said she loved her before?* She bent down and gazed into those dark eyes that seemed to hold a glistening sparkle deep within that she hadn't noticed before.

"You love me?" Gertie said very softly while intently gazing at her young daughter's face.

"Yes, momma, very much!" Setting down her doughnut and ice pack, Salena wrapped her arms about her mother in a big bear hug. Greedy Gertie felt her eyes moisten. *This was too much.*

"Ummm, yes....umm...be good for Matilda, o.k.?" Gertie hastily withdrew from Salena's grasp and headed towards her bedroom where she could hear the whir of the vacuum as Matilda was already busy at work. Wiping her eyes so no one would see the hot tears that were falling, she managed to compose herself enough to yell: "Matilda, Matilda--I'm leaving now", gaining Matilda's attention and receiving back a nod and wave. Greedy Gertie hurried down the hall to the garage door entry wondering what on earth had happened to penetrate her hard shell. *I don't understand, I don't understand,* was all that came to her mind as she closed the door behind her. *How had love found its way into my house?*

Chapter Fourteen

8:00 A.M. found the Ranger showered, shaved and ready to greet the crew of three barking canines at the base of his tower. A second pot of coffee as well as his time spent with the King, had re-energized his spirit, soul and body and Rick the Red-Necked Ranger felt ready to take on the world and the forces that were behind hiding the beloved Kenny the Koala Bear. As he began his descent downward to where Bubba Doo Wah Wah, James the beagle and Gerald, the German shepherd had gathered at the base clearing surrounding the tower, Rick was alive with anticipation that these elite of the Semper Fi Canine Reconnaissance Corps would surely have some good news to report. He quickened his pace with these hopeful thoughts and was soon at ground level to greet his canine troop representatives.

"Good morning, gentlemen of the Elite Corps," the Ranger boomed with a proper salute to show his deep respect for these well-trained warriors in dog flesh. When it was just Bubba and him alone, he was anything but formal, but when others of the Corps were about, he attempted to maintain a modicum of decorum.

"Greetings to you from the Corps and General Sedmeyer, Sr. Ranger of the Pine Valley Forest," answered Bubba Doo Wah Wah with all proper respectful tone of address.

"I am very hopeful of a positive report this morning gentlemen. Please give me some news of breakthrough regarding our koala bear case so I can set a mother's heart at ease today," said the Ranger in lively spirited tones. As he did so, he saw the expression of Corps neutrality in their eyes, so instilled into the forces when they were being reviewed by a superior, to one that clearly showed that a positive report would not be forthcoming this morning at least.

Bubba broke the dismal silence. "Senior Ranger, Sir, I am saddened to report that neither we, nor the Corps, have any news noteworthy to report, sir. However, we are still at work and not all leads have been exhausted yet."

"And what of the feline forces? How is Puss Puss B' Guss Guss faring?"

"I met secretly with the Puss Puss late last night. He relayed to me that the alley cats have been alerted as well as all indoor/outdoor cats. Thus far, no news has been forthcoming regarding seeing Kenny the Koala Bear either inside or outside. But Puss Puss B' Guss Guss assures me all felines will keep their eyes and ears open to anything that could lead us to uncover the whereabouts of the Bear."

"Well, I know those felines are a curious lot and perhaps that will be to our benefit in the uncovering of a clue." The Ranger looked away from the three canines before him, gazing far over their heads to the woods beyond. The three remained at attention as they knew this was the Ranger's way when he was deep in contemplation--particularly when it was a matter of grave concern. He would appear to be oblivious to everything around him, as if he had forgotten that they were even there. Actually, in these moments of silence, the Ranger was more aware of everything about him, including that which could not be seen with visible eyes. He sensed a fight between the warriors of the King and those of the enemy forces, unseen, but afoot nonetheless. These were forebodings that he kept to himself and would only share with his fellow Rangers and at times with Bubba Doo Wah Wah in private. For now though, he shook himself and returned his focus to the earnest three, alert and ready to do his bidding.

"Gentlemen, we must not lose heart, nor grow slack. It is still early in the game yet and still much ground to cover. Keep yourselves alert, aware and armed for battle. We will meet again next

Saturday, 0800 sharp. If there is any breakthrough before that time, you know where to find me. Until then, you are dismissed."

The Ranger turned back towards the tower as Bubba Doo Wah Wah told his compatriots to head onward and that he would catch up with them in a moment. As they bounded up the hill, the Ranger turned, knowing Bubba would still be there. He knelt down on one knee and Bubba came close.

"Be careful, my canine friend," the Ranger warned softly as he affectionately rubbed Bubba's head, "There's a war brewing and we are right smack dab in the thick of it."

Far beyond the horizon of green interspersed with yellows and crimsons of the peaceful Pine Valley Forest where the Ranger had just finished meeting with his most trustworthy alliance of the canine Corps, a dark and sinister meeting of another type had just begun. This meeting was not one that could be seen with the human eyes nor was it taking place where sunlight and laughter could reach. This was a grouping of the dark forces, the ones that the Ranger sensed, and there was anger in the ranks.

"How could you have been so sloppy!" hissed Nocturnicon. "You left her alone with that Bear instead of keeping her riled up with the torments of her delightfully wicked brother and now the enemy's poison has invaded her and she is going about that home singing his infernal praises! Our once solidly selfish, evil, dark Land of Mean now has a crack of the enemy's light shining in it--all because of your slovenliness!" With that epithet, the demon, Nocturnicon, raked his razor claws across the lower ranking Spearnobus' leg causing a howl of pain to bellow forth. The crowd of stinking dark creatures hovering about in this dank, blackened realm of meeting let forth wicked growls of disgust over this terrible revelation that the Land of Mean had been invaded.

"We must recover this lost ground!" Nocturnicon bellowed as he raised up to full stature, towering over his rank, smelly, black as pitch winged forces. "We must practice containment as the enemy's ways are infectious like a disease. If that Bear or that horrid singer of the enemy's songs goes beyond that home, we will be fighting a battle akin to a raging wildfire and that is <u>not</u> going to happen--not on my watch! I am therefore assigning you, Hedgethorn, to keep that Bear from ever leaving that house and Prurient, Grimely and Odiferous, you are to be an ever present guard of the other three Pomposities to keep them stirred up and at odds with that simp Salena who now belongs to the enemy. And, if the chance arises..." Nocturnicon now leaned forward, hot foul breath shooting forth as steam into the twisted faces of the four hosts from hell, "...do in the Bear and that singing sap thus eliminating the light from the Land of Mean and bringing it back under our total domination once more!" A hideous roar of sickly pleasure rose from the evil hoard. "Be gone, all of you from my presence and take heed to do our master's bidding or pay the consequences!" With that, the beastly creatures took flight, hissing and shrieking as they went forth like humongous winged bats in the unseen realm towards the Land of Mean.

Hannah's outburst had brought her parents racing out of the kitchen to see their daughter in a state of high pitched fervor in the family room. The pizza bites that were now out of the oven and sitting on the range top as well as the chocolate milk poured and ready to go on the nearby countertop were of no interest to the nearly hysterical Hannah. She grabbed her mother and father's hands, practically dragging them to her bedroom. She fairly fell upon Puss Puss B' Guss Guss who had settled down for another nap on her soft quilted bedspread.

"See, see--look at his paw! Pine sap! This proves he was in the woods! It proves it!" Hannah dropped Puss Puss B' Guss Guss into her mother's arms, and then held up the hind paw in question for her to inspect. "And, look, dad, look!" Hannah was now gesturing wildly towards the window behind the kitty tree, "Muddy dog prints--these must be from the dog that carried Puss Puss on his back in the knapsack!" Daniel Stillwaters went to the window that his daughter was so frantically gesturing towards for closer inspection.

Hannah kept bobbing from her mother on the bed with Puss Puss B' Guss Guss to her father who was looking out the window. She kept exclaiming: "This proves it, this proves it!!!" Daniel Stillwaters turned from his window inspection to his hysterically excited daughter. "Hannah, my dear daughter, calm down, calm down," he said gently but firmly as he placed his arms about her once more in typical daddy bear hug fashion.

Hannah wrestled free from her dad's arms. "Calm down? Daddy, this proves I didn't imagine it! Puss Puss B' Guss Guss was in the woods that day with the dog that left these paw prints. He was there! With all those other dogs! So was Uncle Rick! Let's call him. He knows--he'll tell you!"

"Now, Hannah, you have to stop this excitement or you are going to end up back at the hospital," said Judith in true concerned mother fashion.

"But, mom, we have to call Uncle Rick right now!"

"Hannah," Daniel Stillwaters' tone had turned from one of loving father to that of sternness. "You need to stop this right now and listen to your mother. I want you to simmer down and get into your bed here and your mom will bring you your pizza snack."

As Hannah began another protest, the look from her father quenched it. She turned back her covers and crawled under them pulling them about her for comfort. "I'm sorry daddy, momma..it's just that...."

"Hannah, we will talk about this at another time when you are more rested. Please settle down for now," implored momma Judith. Seeing the downcast expression on her daughter's face, she added,

"Look, I promise you we will talk about it tomorrow after we have all had a good night's rest. Your father and I are exhausted, as I am sure you are. Let's just relax the rest of this day, have a peaceful evening and give it until another day, o.k.?"

Hannah noticed for the first time how very tired both of her parents looked. Though she so wanted to solve this mystery now, her love for them combined with the desire to please her King won out.

"O.K., mom, dad, I'll give it a rest... for now."

"That's my girl." Dad's tone had resumed its natural jovialness. "Momma--how about those pizza bites? We've got a starving cub here!"

Chapter Fifteen

As soon as Salena heard the telltale click of the door confirming momma Gertie's departure, she hopped down from the kitchen stool placing the ice bag next to her half-eaten doughnut. Rounding the corner to the hallway, she could still hear Matilda vacuuming in her parents' bedroom. Feet like wings carried her down the hall to Horatio's room to get the desk chair that she would need to reach the attic stairs button. It took her a bit of doing to drag it down the carpeted hallway as she was not as tall and strong as Horatio, but she managed to set it in place. Salena had to stand on tippy toes to reach the attic stairs button. Such joy and anticipation arose within her small being as the stairs descended from the secluded world above. She bounded up them as quickly as her short legs would go into the musty dark attic. This time around, she felt no fear of the darkness as she reached for the light switch at the top to the right. Light flooded the formerly hidden attic realm and Salena pushed the button for the stairs to close encapsulating her away from her ordinary world below. The precious moments that she had awaited all week to spend with Kenny the Koala Bear could now begin.

She raced to the trunk, drawing forth the key she had kept so carefully hidden in her Fairy Princess doll's purse in the bottom of her toy chest all week and now, with shaking hands, inserted it in the antique trunk. With a quick turn and loud click, she opened the trunk home of her precious koala bear friend.

There he was--bright, radiant, warm eyes staring up at her as he lay on his back atop the colorful patterned quilt, a sharp contrast to his deep chocolate brown fur. He raised his arms expectantly to her, and she scooped him up with fervor into a big warm hug as she twirled about with him.

"Welcome back, dear Salena! I have missed you so," said the Bear.

"Oh, Kenny, I am so sorry it has taken a whole week to get back to you, but this is the first chance I have had to come see you! My mom and Horatio are away from the house at his clarinet lesson."

"Are you home all by yourself?"

"No, our maid, Matlida, is downstairs cleaning. But the important thing is that I am here with you and soo happy!" Salena plopped down on the large pillows placing Kenny the Koala Bear on a pillow right next to her.

"Have you been happy this week, little one?"

"Oh, yes, Kenny, more than ever before--and, I have been singing the song you taught me too--over and over and over again!" Salena's eyes lit up with a sparkly glow as she told Kenny about her week.

"Do your mom and dad like your song too?" queried Kenny.

Salena paused. "Well daddy wasn't quite sure what to make of it, but, momma...well...it seemed to make her angry." The sparkle had faded from her eyes as she relayed this part of her week to Kenny and her gaze turned downward. "Why does it make momma mad, Kenny?" she said sadly and softly. "Am I doing something wrong?"

The koala bear gently raised her chin up with his paw so that Salena again gazed into those wise knowing eyes. "No, little one. You are not doing anything wrong. You see, there are two kingdoms and everyone either belongs to one or the other."

"Two kingdoms?"

"Yes, sweet girl. You see, last week when you asked the King of Kings to come into your heart and to make you all beautiful inside like a diamond shining in the sun, you went from the Kingdom of Darkness into the Kingdom of Light. That is why you have such joy in your heart now and why you love to sing praises to the King. His Kingdom is much more powerful than the Kingdom of Darkness and it is filled with joy and gladness. Those who follow Him are well cared for and protected and loved by Him both now, and forever more."

"But, Kenny, I don't understand. Why doesn't everyone want to live in the Kingdom of Light if it is the best kingdom? Why would anyone want to live in the Kingdom of Darkness?"

"Young one, that is because the Kingdom of Darkness has a ruler as well--<u>not</u> powerful like our king, but he practices what is called deception. Actually, you could call him the master of deception."

"Deception?" What's that?"

"Simply put--he is very good at telling lies and tricking people into believing that the lies are true. This is what keeps most people in the Kingdom of Darkness. They have believed a lie, or a bunch of lies. It is only when something happens in their life that doesn't fit with the lie anymore that they may wake up so to speak to see that they are in the wrong kingdom. Then, they can switch kingdoms like you did by asking the King of Kings to come into their heart, and follow Him for the rest of their lives and never ever go back to that dark kingdom again."

"Then, Kenny, is that why momma gets so angry when I sing that special song you taught me? Because she lives in the Kingdom of Darkness?"

Kenny the Koala Bear saw the sadness and struggle reflected in Salena's eyes as her mind grappled with this disturbing new truth. But it was a freeing truth and one that the King had assured him that even this little girl would be able to comprehend as time progressed. He placed his paw gently on her hand resting near him as he replied softly: "Yes, young one, this is why the song makes your momma angry."

"I don't want momma to be angry, Kenny! I want her to be happy. I want her to be in the Kingdom of Light like me--how can I make her change kingdoms so she can be happy and not mad all the time?"

"Well, dear child, that is something that the King will show you day by day as you stay close to Him. You can't make someone switch kingdoms though. The King of Kings never forces someone to do something they don't want to do. But, what He does do is He uses precious vessels like you to cause His light to brightly shine through them. Others will see it and become so attracted to the light that their heart becomes filled with a desire to change. So--all you need to be concerned with right now, little one, is to be an overflowing vessel of His love and His light. He will take care of the rest of it. Here is a sure saying from Him to you to treasure in your heart:

> *Trust in the Lord with all of thine heart; and*
> *Lean not unto thine own understanding.*
> *In all of thy ways acknowledge Him, and*
> *He shall direct thy paths. (Prov. 3:5-6)*

The sparkle had returned to young Salena's eyes as she said: "One more question, Kenny--what's a vessel?"

Kenny the Koala Bear gave a playful poke at Salena's tummy as he answered: "You are, beautiful girl--and I bet you are good at tag because....you are it!" And the Bear quickly scampered across the dusty attic floor as Salena, giggling with gleeful abandon, gave chase.

The delicious smell of bacon sizzling in one pan while blueberry pancakes puffed to perfection atop the griddle on the burner nearby wafted their aromatic fragrances to the still dreaming Hannah. Her small frame was nestled cozily in a half circle beneath the soft quilted covers of her white wrought iron, twin bed. Puss Puss B' Guss Guss was in his own kitty dreamland snuggled in the crook of his owner's bent legs. As the scent of breakfast began to rouse Hannah, her legs moved beneath the covers and the Puss Puss' second nap of the morning was disturbed. He gave a slightly disgruntled *meowr* and jumped down from the bed as Hannah sleepily stretched her form still more asleep than awake. Puss Puss' claws plucking loudly against the sisal rope of his kitty tree caused Hannah to open a heavy lidded eye in his direction. "Morning, Puss Puss," she yawned, turning her body towards him. He responded with his typical flopsker routine, plopping down on his side and rolling onto his back, bountiful fluffy white belly exposed, paws curled up near his chin in his adorable "how could you possibly resist petting me?" repose.

"Ooh, you soo know that you're cute," cooed Hannah as she pulled her legs from beneath the covers and sat up for another stretch on the side of her bed. She felt stiff and awkward with her arm in the cast but nothing could keep her from getting down on the floor with her beloved Puss Puss B' Guss Guss to give him his belly loves and kisses in the crook of his bunny rabbit soft fur on his neck. Rumbling purrs of kitty delight were the soothing and reassuring symphony for Hannah's ears this early a.m.

"Ahh, Puss Puss, if only you could talk and tell me what really happened that day in the woods--I know I didn't imagine it!" Hannah let out a soft sigh and put her head gently on Puss Puss B' Guss Guss' side. The rumbling grew louder and Hannah's mind relaxed with the comforting sound in her fur pressed ear. The rhythmic purr might have lulled her off to dreamland once more on the plush carpet floor of her bedroom if her father's head had not poked around the corner that very moment with his deep voiced "Breakfast's ready--rise and shine--those who sleep, weep!" in typical teasing dad fashion.

"I'll be back, Puss Puss," Hannah said, righting herself carefully by putting her main weight on her good arm.

By the time she reached the kitchen, Hannah's mom and dad were already seated and awaiting her. The breakfast fare of blueberry pancakes, crisp bacon and warm maple syrup filled the table. Mom and dad's large-mugged coffee cups had steam rising out of them while Hannah's favorite tulip glass was filled to the brim with orange juice and crushed ice, just the way she liked it. A vase of lavender and white roses was in the center of it all. Mom and dad's unison of "Morning, sleepyhead," was a caress of warm family love that Hannah relished as she slipped into her seat and hands joined while heads bowed and thanksgiving rose to the heavens with gratitude to the King of Kings and Lord of Lords for her safe return home and for the bounty set before them.

Silverware jangled as napkins were placed in laps. Plates were filled and hungry appetites appeased with the delicious homemade breakfast as cheerful banter erupted between the members of this very grateful family. Quiet ensued for a few moments as each slowed down in satisfaction from the meal. Hannah looked at her parents' smiles and relaxation that had replaced last night's tiredness and tension and thought that now might be a good time to broach the subject of her woods' experience. She was markedly mistaken as her questions about Puss Puss B' Guss Guss and the dogs being in the woods caused a darkened cloud of sadness and exasperation to come across her parents' features. The sunshine smiles abruptly vanished.

"Hannah," said Daniel Stillwaters in a solemn tone, "I think we need to talk very seriously about this and I need you to listen to me very carefully."

The jovial father was replaced by one that Hannah very much respected, but, still she was struggling desperately not to argue with. Daniel Stillwaters sensed that his daughter was uncomfortable due to her squirming in her chair, and he strove to keep his tone soft, yet firm.

"I want you to be very quiet for a few moments and simply listen--don't interrupt. I have some things to say and when I am done, I will give you a chance to speak. O.k.?"

Hannah nodded, eyes fixed on her father.

"Now--I understand that this has been a very traumatic experience for you and I want you to understand that it has been an equally traumatic experience for your mother and I on a level that you will probably not be able to understand until you become a parent yourself." Hannah's dad lovingly placed his hand on Hannah's cast as he continued: "And, my dear Hannah, I would rather that my arm had been broken than to have had you go through this pain. What I want to talk about first though is this: we, as your parents, set up certain rules to try and keep you safe, as you well know, right?"

Again, Hannah nodded.

"Our rules for camping have always been that you are <u>not</u> ever, under <u>any</u> circumstance, to venture off from our campsite without one of us with you, is that not correct?"

"Yes, daddy, but...," Hannah said.

Daniel Stillwaters stopped her, mid sentence. "No, Hannah, there is no "but". You knew the rule. The rule is there to keep you from danger that could occur in the forest. Many things could happen. And something very, very serious <u>did</u> happen. If your mother or I had been with you, you would not have been up in that tree, out on a thin limb, which gave way under your weight. We would not have allowed you to climb up into that tree. And, then, none of this would have happened."

"But I wouldn't have gone up in the tree if I hadn't heard all those dogs barking and then I had to go up really high to see where they were and I didn't know the branch was so thin and I saw Puss Puss and Uncle Rick and..."

"You could have been killed, Hannah!" interjected Judith Stillwaters, with the sound of tears in her voice. "You, my precious girl, could have died!"

And with that exclamation Judith got up from the table and knelt down next to Hannah. "Don't you understand what your father is saying? You want to talk about some foolishness with your Puss Puss, an indoor cat that never goes outside and packs of dogs in the woods and Uncle Rick right in the middle of that nonsensical fantasy! Hannah, come back to planet earth! What we are trying to get across to you is that if you had stayed in obedience to the rules that we have set for our camping trips, we could have had a lovely time! Our first evening was so great and it would have continued onward into the weekend and instead, we almost lost you!" Hannah's mom stood and drew Hannah up from her chair and close into her arms. "I don't know what I would do if I ever lost you, my baby girl--I don't know if I could get through that--you are so precious to your father and I!". Judith's words came out in sobs as she cuddled her daughter close to her. Hannah's eyes as well filled with hot, moist tears. Words gave way to the sounds of soft sobbing as Judith clung tightly to Hannah. As the sobs between mother and daughter lessened, Daniel Stillwaters' strong voice, now slightly muted, continued and Judith released Hannah so she could again look at her father as he spoke.

"My daughter, my dear Hannah! I love you and your mom loves you with all the capability we have as human beings to love you. That is also why we have rules. To show you our love through directions that will keep you safe. Do you know who loves you even more than us, though?"

"God does," said Hannah quietly.

"Yes, exactly, my girl. And one of God's commandments is that you honor your parents. One of the ways you show that is by being obedient to what they tell you to do. When you are disobedient to them, you are breaking one of God's commandments. When you do so, you are also being disobedient to God. Disobedience is also called rebellion. Rebellion can never be blessed by God. When you disobeyed us, you were where we could not protect you. Rebellion places you in the enemy's camp as you have rejected God's protection as well. Do you understand how serious this is, Hannah? We don't want this to become a pattern in your life as you have a tender, sensitive heart with many beautiful gifts that God has given you. The way for all the blessings and good things that God has for you is to stay obedient to Him, as well as to us as your parents because He has placed us in authority over you to lead you and guide you in His ways. When you have done wrong, you need to have a heart that is quick to repent. To say, "I'm sorry". First, to Him. And then to those you have hurt by your wrong actions."

Daniel Stillwaters' gaze seemed to pierce directly into Hannah's heart. She felt as though the Lord Himself was speaking in a way that caused her heart to break over the hurt she had caused.

"Oh, daddy, mommy--I am so sorry--please forgive me!"

This time, both mom and dad enveloped their beautiful girl and soon a family of three were on their knees, in prayer, a young one restored through the miracle of repentance and forgiveness. The unseen glorious angels rejoiced. And equally unseen, defeated demons hissed. And a family was back on track in unity under the King of Kings' mighty hand of protection.

Chapter Sixteen

Light flooding the attic as the stairs descended to the hallway below startled Salena from her game of chase with Kenny. The cavernous opening to the world below caused the horrible realization that someone had pushed the button to the stairs from down there and would soon ascend to where she and Kenny had so gleefully been romping only moments before. Salena froze. Kenny, however, moving quick as lightning, hopped, skipped and then gave one final jump and into the trunk he landed. "Salena, shut the lid." Salena, trying to ignore the thumping, approaching footsteps from the stairs below, skittered across the floor at Kenny the Koala Bear's urgent command, gave a last loving smile at her bear friend, and hastily closed the trunk and locked it. Just as she jammed the key back into her jean pocket, she saw Matilda's face appear.

"Little girl, what doing here? You scare Matilda. No find you anywhere. Call and call and call. Come here now. Way from dirty things. Momma have fit."

Salena, who had lost track of time in this wonderful attic world, ran to grab Matilda about her legs.

"Oh, Matilda, please, please don't be mad at me. I'm sorry for not telling you where I was. It's just..."

"It's just--this is your, how you say--secret place?"

"Yes, my secret place!" exclaimed Salena joyfully.

"Matilda understand now--when I was little girl, I play in place where no one know--all mine--away from brothers and sisters bother me--you too--away from brother bother you, no?"

"Yes, Matilda. I need this place to play alone."

"Well, little girl. Tell you what. If you don't mess anything up, and you tell me where you are, you can play here when momma and brother away, o.k.? But--promise--no break things, right?"

"I promise--and please don't tell them, o.k.?"

"O.k.--I understand little girl world--let's go down now before they come home."

Salena, grateful for Matilda's tender understanding, took Matilda's outstretched hand, and descended the stairs, back to the seemingly ordinary, ordered world that was the Pomposity household. Unbeknownst to both Matilda and Salena, however, were the four unsavory characters from the enemy's camp, which had just made their entrance in the unseen realm of this home. The battle between the Kingdom of Light and the Kingdom of Darkness was about to begin.

As Kenny's warm charcoal eyes adjusted to the darkness of his trunk world, an uneasiness seemed to settle over his spirit like a dark thunder cloud blocking out the sun's radiance on a storm struck afternoon. A sense of impending doom. Dread perhaps? No, this was darker. This was pure evil. A sharp chill shuddered through his body. Something was terribly amiss outside of his safe, trunk world. Usually, Kenny felt the enveloping of the King about his being, but not now. Every sense in Kenny was on high alert. He pressed his ear to one side of the trunk and strained to hear something, anything, as the evil foreboding presence grew stronger. A foul smell caused his nostrils to twitch; the odor was seeping through the keyhole. Kenny shivered as he pulled the quilt about his soft furry body, barely breathing, sensing the evil, dark presence drawing closer. And then abruptly, he heard the wicked chatter, causing him to remain rigidly motionless.

"Well, here we are at last, comrades of darkness," hissed Hedgethorn, "Let's find that bear and have ourselves a grand time of terror."

"I say we scope the house first to mess with the humans," said Prurient.

"No, let's do a bit of mischief where we're at to make them nervous," chimed in Odiferous.

"I'm for waiting until nightfall when they're all home--and deal with them all at once," grunted Grimely.

The four demons on assignment were an ugly crew. Mottled leather-like skin, long razor sharp claws, wings that folded behind their backs when at rest and then expanded like a bat's except a thousand times larger, eyes that were yellow with red glowing centers. These were beings from the worst nightmare that a human could ever imagine. Except these were not fantasy creatures. These were real beings that were under the total control of the Kingdom of Darkness and its ruler.

As beautiful and majestic as was the Heavenly realm, the Kingdom of Light, this realm, existent in the pits of the earth, was its direct, dank, foul opposite with everything ugly imaginable as well as beyond imaginable, within its blackened borders. The rancid banter between the demons of evil grew louder and more fierce as each demon shrilly asserted his idea on the direction to take within the Pomposity home. Kenny listened in silent horror within his still secure trunk world to the plots and schemes of these wicked creatures of the underworld. Fear began to grip his heart as he thought about his sweet, tender and unaware friend Salena and her family being at danger and risk of harm from the enemy's camp. He felt so helpless and almost gave way to panic. Then it happened. Deep from within the recesses of his heart and mind came the words: *"For God hath not given us the spirit of fear but of power, and of love, and of a sound mind." (2 Tim.1:7)*. As these words filled his being, his heart stopped beating so rapidly, and his mind cleared and panic flew away like a butterfly flitting from a flower petal. Then, Kenny remembered two more scriptures that gave him great courage and comfort: *"... If thou canst believe, all things are possible to him that believeth."* (Mark 9:23), and *"For the weapons of our warfare are not carnal, but mighty through God to the pulling down of strong holds;"(2 Cor. 10:4).*

Kenny spoke in a whisper so that the evil intruders could not hear, but it was in a spirit firm in the faith of what his King of Kings could do. "Dear precious Father in Heaven, I come to you in the name that is above every name--the name at which every knee will bow and every tongue will confess, and I pray for His protection right now for my dear friend Salena who belongs to you, Lord, and for her family, who so desperately need to know you, and, I ask right now that these demons be vanquished from this place. O precious Father! Please send your mighty angels to do battle on behalf of your servant. Thank you my King! Amen!"

As Kenny concluded his prayer, he could still hear the bone-chilling shrieking and hissing of the demons as they carried on their arguments of evil. They seemed to be getting closer to the trunk as well because the odor was growing stronger and to the point where he almost felt nauseous. He was startled as he heard a thud and then a loud drumming on the top of his trunk. Could it be? He shuddered realizing the thud was more than likely one of the demons plopped on top of his trunk with its claw-like fingers drumming in succession as it sat there.

Kenny's breathing was very shallow, but he refused to give in to fear now. *I have prayed and my King will answer me,* he resolutely reassured himself. It was the longest moment of this courageous little bear's life--but it truly was but a moment (though seeming to Kenny like an eternity had passed) when all of a sudden a beam of light flashed through the key hole and Kenny the Koala Bear heard the clank of steel against steel outside his trunk together with wails and sickening moans coming from the demon intruders. Kenny dared to put his eye to the trunk keyhole and the sight that greeted his eyes brought awe mingled with glee and a sense of triumph to his tender bear heart. Before him stood four angels arrayed resplendently in glorious raiment, light emanating from the very fiber of their beings. They were beautiful beyond description as well as enormously tall and broad of form. They towered over the four emissaries from hell and the swords of the demons fell in short order to the ground as the glistening powerful swords of the angelic host far outmatched them. The battle was as swift as it was furious as the angelic host sent the defeated, screeching demons straight through the attic wall to the outdoors as both forces vanished beyond Kenny's view. It was like a scene from a movie. But Kenny the Koala Bear knew it was real and that he had been given the rare privilege to see into the unseen realm by viewing with his own eyes the defeat of the enemy in answer to prayer.

Peace flooded Kenny's soul as he lay his little bear head back on the pillow and comforter in his once again dimly lit trunk home. Joy and thanksgiving filled his heart as well as he sang praise to His King.

"I will bless the Lord at all times: His praise shall continually be in my mouth. My soul shall make her boast in the Lord: the humble shall hear thereof, and be glad. O magnify the Lord with me, and let us exalt his name together. I sought the Lord, and he heard me, and delivered me from all my fears. They looked unto him, and were lightened: and their faces were not ashamed. This poor man cried, and the Lord heard him, and saved him out of all his troubles. The angel of the Lord encampeth round about them who fear him, and delivereth them. O taste and see that the Lord is good: blessed is the man that trusteth in him. O fear the Lord, ye his saints: for there is no want to them that fear him. The young lions do lack, and suffer hunger: but they that seek the Lord shall not want any good thing. Come, ye children, hearken unto me: I will teach you the fear of the Lord. What man is he that desireth life, and loveth many days,

that he may see good? Keep thy tongue from evil, and thy lips from speaking guile. Depart from evil, and do good; seek peace, and pursue it. The eyes of the Lord are upon the righteous, and his ears are open unto their cry. The face of the Lord is against them who do evil, to cut off the remembrance of them from the Earth. The righteous cry, and the Lord heareth, and delivereth them out of all their troubles. The Lord is nigh unto them that are of a broken heart; and saveth such as be of a contrite spirit. Many are the afflictions of the righteous: but the Lord delivereth him out of them all. He keepeth all his bones: not one of them is broken. Evil shall kill the wicked: and they that hate the righteous shall be desolate. The Lord redeemeth the soul of his servants: and none of them who trust in him shall be desolate." (Psalm 34)

Kenny fell asleep to this song of Praise and his thanksgiving was well received on high. Unbeknownst to Kenny, however, was the fact that the Angelic host were <u>still</u> encamped outside the Pomposity home--swords held high--glistening in the now darkened star-lit sky--each one keeping post at the respective four corners of the rooftop of the house. Angelic soldiers of the King--on guard and alert, awaiting further instructions from on High.

Chapter Seventeen

Pugnacious Pomposity, III was flying high--high that is, in the thoughts he had about himself and how wonderfully awesome and incredibly brilliant he was. He could barely keep his mind on the monotony of driving home as he thought back to the announcement today from the dean of the College of Arts and Sciences that he was to receive the prestigious arachnid researcher of the year award at a banquet, black tie affair, of course, in the ballroom of the Civic Center, downtown Land of Mean. His work had been singled out over a thousand other such researchers in the country. For certain, an article would be done on him for his favorite magazine, possibly even with his photo. Maybe even a television interview. *Oh, will Gertie be pleased!* A chance for her to shine in the new diamond necklace he had recently purchased anticipating just such an occasion. *Of course, she will probably insist on a new dress, but, that was Gertie to the T.* The idea of more expense being shelled out to match his ego with his picture perfect wife was a small price to pay. *Oh, what a glorious event this will be,* he mused as the automatic garage door opened the way to his cavernous garage.

Slamming the car door with a little hop like a silly school boy with a new toy, he burst through the door, shouting, "Gertie, Gertie--where are you? Come quickly--I have great news!"

"What is it, Pugnacious? I'm in the bedroom," bellowed a grumpy Gertie who had parked herself on the pillow ensconced window seat overlooking the patio. She remained shaken and reflective from her last mother-daughter encounter and Salena's tender expression of love towards her. *Love.* A most troubling concept to Gertie. Money: she understood--the more, the better. Jewelry: expensive and lots of it. Clothes: the flowing gowns and furs provoking jealousy in other women. Prestige: living in a fancy neighborhood with a husband who was frequently honored at the university. An elite lifestyle that placed them above the common folk in every sense of the word. All of this she relished, understood and was exceedingly comfortable and familiar in. But, *love? What was that?* It provoked her, prodded at her, caused hidden and buried emotions to stir--distant memories wanting to surface, and she didn't like it one bit. She felt edgy, out of control, *must push it away--can't have tears again like that day...*

"Gertie, Gertie?

Oh, why is he still hollering. "What?!"

Pugnacious Pomposity, III rounded the corner of the elegant bedroom to find a terribly distressed Greedy Gertie stretched out on the window seat with plump pillows surrounding her. "What's the matter, dear Gertie," Pugnacious said in a perfunctory tone, not at all expecting an answer, "I have such auspicious news to relay!"

Greedy Gertie rolled her eyes, pushing her bony fingers into the lush, royal blue velvet cushion to straighten herself to a more erect sitting position. Heaving an exasperated sigh with sarcasm dripping off each word, she retorted, "Do tell, I am all ears."

Pugnacious needed no encouragement to brag upon himself or his accomplishments. With chest puffed out, head tilted upward, and strutting about the bedroom like a peacock in full display of his feathers, he raved: "Well, my dear, it's like this...your husband, after being reviewed among thousands of professors throughout the country in a process that has involved some of the most notable minds in the land, I have been selected to receive the prestigious Arcus Award and named the Arachnid Researcher of the Year!"

Gertie, nonplussed, continued her non-interested stare in Pugnacious' direction. "And...what do you get? A trophy with a spider on the top of it?"

Pugnacious Pomposity, III snorted. "Really, Gertie, you are the most trying woman sometimes! I am sure I will get a most appropriate award, not something so gauche as you have described." He came closer to her now, grabbing her hands and pulling her to her feet. With a dance like twirl, he continued, "Gertie, this means a black tie affair at the ballroom of the Civic Center--you, in an elegant evening gown with the new diamond necklace I bought you gracing your lovely neck. Fine wine, elegant food, dancing 'til the wee hours. Most likely, the press will be there. Photos for magazines and the newspaper--it will truly be a night to remember for us. And, most likely, monetary compensation to boot. A promotion. Maybe enough for that new car you have been wanting?"

At the mention of all these treasures that made up Gertie's world, she suddenly felt more like her greedy self again. Now, she <u>was</u> excited! "When will this wonderful event be?"

"Two weeks from this Saturday. Of course, we will need to find a sitter for Horatio and Salena as this is an adult-only event. Black tie affair, you know."

The smile vanished from Greedy Gertie's face. She let go of her husband's hands as he had been mock ballroom dancing her about the bedroom. She slumped to the bed.

"What's wrong now, Gertie?"

"Well...it's just that...well..."

"Well...what?

"Well...no one wants to watch our kids, Pugnacious!"

"What do you mean, no one? How about Adrienne?"

"No."

"Jennifer?"

"No."

"Felicity?"

"No."

"Holly? She's really good with kids."

"No."

"Well, you will have to find someone, Gertie. Maybe someone who doesn't know them?"

Greedy Gertie fumed, "Everyone knows our kids, Pugnacious. And I have exhausted the list. The last time we went out, that was the last new babysitter. And she vowed she would never come back. I have no idea who to call."

Pugnacious was not willing to let the wind sailing his pompous sailboat on waves of grandeur to deflate over such a trifling matter as a babysitter. *With a mind like mine, I will solve this silly issue.* He gazed in deep reflection in the mirror, admiring what he perceived as chiseled, intelligent features. The light bulb went on just as he knew it would.

"Hannah Stillwaters. She would be perfect. Call her forthwith--problem solved!" Without waiting for a reply from Gertie, he turned on his heel to go find Horatio and Salena to give them the good news of their father's accolade.

Greedy Gertie was glad he had gone. *My, I am in a pickle. The very girl I told to never come back to our home is the very one now who I will have to convince to come or it will be my head for sure!*

The delicious aroma of bread baking in the oven must be what Heaven smells like, thought Hannah as she swung her legs back and forth in rhythmic motion perched at the kitchen counter stool impatiently awaiting the *ding* of the timer that would cause momma Stillwaters to bring forth golden loaves of goodness, one of which would be sliced and swathed with butter while still warm, a treat Hannah's taste buds relished more than the sweetest candy. It had been a busy morning of baking for Hannah's mom and the warm, sunlit kitchen showed it sporting doughy bowls, floured bread board, a sink filled with measuring and mixing utensils, and a light flour dusting just about everywhere including Hannah's nose from getting it too close to the bowl for a scent of yeasty, egg-rich dough. Though Hannah couldn't help her mom due to her casted arm, she stayed close by her, enjoying the bread making process. The push pull rhythm used in the kneading process was strangely soothing with the *boom thwacka* sound echoing throughout the house as Mrs. Stillwaters zestily threw the dough ball onto the floured bread board.

It was now close to lunch time and Hannah's stomach was rumbling as she anticipated with eagerness the countdown to gastronomical heaven. Almost like an orchestrated symphony, the *ding* of the oven timer was met by the lilting melody of Mrs. Stillwaters' cell phone on the counter. "Hannah, could you get that?" said Judith Stillwaters, oven mitts on both hands, busily engaged in pulling bread sheets filled with shiny, golden brown, braided loaves from the oven.

"Sure, momma...Stillwaters residence, Hannah speaking," she politely said upon grasping the cell phone with her good hand. Hannah's eyes grew large with surprise as the caller identified herself. "Momma, it's Gertie Pomposity." Hannah spoke in a hush with her hand over the mouthpiece.

"Tell her I'll be right with her." Judith deftly transferred the steaming bread from the oven pans to the cooling racks. Before taking the phone from her daughter's extended hand, she quickly sliced a piece of warm bread for Hannah complete with a pat of creamery butter.

"Yes, Gertie--how are you today?...Really? Oh, just doing some baking. And yourself?...well, yes, she has done some neighborhood babysitting...very much so...all the kids have enjoyed her...when did you say? Two weeks from tomorrow? Five o'clock 'til eleven? She won't need to make dinner? Her arm is still in a cast, you know. Pizza brought in? That sounds good...well, let me talk with her and my husband. Can I call you back this evening? O.k., will do--bye for now."

Hannah could hardly believe the conversation with Gertie Pomposity overheard on this end of the phone.

"Well, my dear...what do you think? Up for some babysitting in the Land of Mean?"

"Seriously, mom? After the way she practically threw me out of her house the last time I was there? Did she even mention that? Did she even apologize?"

Hannah's mom gazed thoughtfully at her daughter as she vented her exasperation over this new proposal of Gertie's.

"And what did she offer to pay? Knowing her, probably not much. I don't know if there is a fee high enough to babysit those little brats..."

"Hold on now, my dear daughter. Back up a bit." Pulling up a stool beside Hannah, she looked directly into those perplexed green eyes. "No, you do not have to babysit if you don't want to. And yes, to your questions--she was extremely, might I add, excessively apologetic about your last encounter. She said that you would not need to make dinner, that she would have pizza ordered in and that she would pay double your going hourly rate just to earn your business. She actually sounded a bit desperate, Hannah. Of course, it's still your decision."

"She really said she was sorry?"

"Yes, she did. Knowing Gertie, it may be very temporary, I know, but, I think we all need the benefit of the doubt until proved otherwise, don't you?"

Hannah met her mother's gaze and then looked down. She thought about recent events and the love of a mom and dad so quick to forgive her.

"You're right, mom...as usual...and maybe, it won't be too bad. They probably will be in bed by nine so that's really only four hours to fill. Maybe I could take one of our good movies over to make the time pass quickly."

"That sounds more like my girl. Let's get some lunch going and get this mess cleaned up, o.k.?"

Chapter Eighteen

T he early morning hours in Pine Valley Forest were always a favorite time for the Ranger. The silence of the nighttime forest gave way to the melodic morning songs of birds that greeted the dawn. The dark night changed to an array of pastel pinks, yellows and oranges as the sun rose over the ridge of the forest line. The first sip of hot roasted coffee warmed Rick the Red-Necked Ranger's soul as he would spend his time in solace and communion with the King of Kings.

But this morning, solace was hard to find. Instead, the Ranger felt heaviness and sadness coupled with frustration as he set his cell phone back onto the rustic log table. He had just spoken with Kenny the Koala Bear's mother after yet another unfruitful meeting with Bubba Doo Wah Wah and the Special Forces at 0800 this morning. Having to tell a tearful Katie Koala that there was still no news of her dear son Kenny had taken its toll on the gentle heart strings of the Ranger. He had been so hopeful that this morning surely there would be news--but absolutely nothing had been gathered from any of the animal forces: canine, feline or koala. Not only was this vexing to the Ranger in the natural, but, he continued to sense a foreboding in his spirit. Something was afoot. He knew a battle was raging behind the scenes, behind what could be seen. And again, the Ranger knelt down to receive direction from on high.

The early morning light caused the Koala Bear's fur to shine in deep mahogany richness and lit up the sparkling hazel eyes of young Salena, so rapt in attention to what the Koala was sharing with her as she sat cross-legged and comfortable on a paisley print cushion across from her new best friend in their secret attic world. The clarinet lessons that Gertie took Horatio to on Saturday mornings gave Salena that precious treasured time with Kenny the Koala Bear where everything else seemed to fade away and this became the only reality that mattered.

"Oh, Kenny, I hope you will stay here forever and teach me all about the Kingdom. I am so happy and at peace when I am here with you!"

"Well, little one, as much as I love being here with you and teaching you about the King of Kings, there are many more who must hear about Him too. So, even when it comes time for me to go, you must carry on here and teach all who will have ears to hear the wonderful message about who He is. Do you agree to do that, little one? It is so very important."

A clouded look came across young Salena's eyes. "But, if you go away, Kenny, how will I be able to learn all about the King? And who will listen to me? I am just a little girl!"

Kenny the Koala Bear's eyes glowed with a warmth that erased all fear and doubt from Salena's heart as he said softly, "The King said that the Kingdom belongs to such as you, young one--and, His Spirit lives in you now and will continue to teach you ALL things--as you stay close to Him and seek His wisdom daily, as I have taught you to do."

Kenny gently took both of the little girl's hands in his paws and with that intense, deep knowing gaze stated firmly, "And...because you have a new nature in you now, it's time for a new name to go with it, one that has been written down in the King's Book regarding you. You are no more to be known as Salena the Shrieker--that was the old you--now, your King calls you....*Sallie the Singer of Songs!*"

Salena lit up with a grin from ear to ear as she was dubbed with her new name--and strangely, it felt like who she really was now. She responded with a big hug for the soft koala bear. "That's an awesome name, Kenny. I hope I can live up to it!"

"With His Grace, you will little one, with His Grace you will!" Kenny paused for a moment, not quite sure if he should tell her. "I believe you will have many more songs from Him to sing."

Formerly Salena the Shrieker, now Sallie the Singer of Songs' eyes grew large. "Really, Kenny?"

"Yes, Sallie. He always gives good gifts to His children and each one in His Kingdom has special gifts and a part to play that only they can do."

Sallie looked reflective. In a voice just above a whisper, she said, "Do you think that my family will hear my songs and want to know the King too?"

Kenny the Koala Bear paused before He spoke. "That is something you will have to leave in the King's hands, little one. You just sing the songs. Trust Him. Believe in Him. Rest in Him. He will take care of it. Just *sing the songs.*"

Sallie the Singer of Songs looked intently at the fluffy chocolate brown koala bear while letting his words wash over her like refreshing spray from a crashing ocean wave on a beach, feeling that this was all so very important yet not really grasping it all either.

"I know this is a lot to take in at once, young Sallie. Don't worry. He will lead you each day. Every day with the King is like a new adventure. All you have to do is follow!"

Sallie the Singer of Songs smiled a mischievous smile at her bear, gave him a playful tag and squealed, "Now you follow me--tag--you're it!"

Seriousness gave way to giggles and romping throughout the musty attic world. Little did they realize, it would be the last time of carefree play.

"Sick? Are you sure? You couldn't come for just an hour for a little light cleaning? That bad, huh...yes, I know you're always here every Saturday...first time in a year. I understand. It's just we are having a sitter over Saturday night...have a big award banquet to go to...oh, I know, one can't help when one gets ill...well, get lots of rest. See you the following Saturday, right? More than likely...ok...bye, Matilda." Gertie threw the phone on the bed. *Really,* she fumed. *So hard to get good help these days.* The week had gone much too slowly for Gertie and now that Friday was finally here with tomorrow being the big gala where she would be the talk of the Land of Mean elite in her new dress and diamond necklace, Gertie wanted the house to be picture perfect before going out Saturday evening. *Drat that Matilda. Too late to call a back up cleaner this late in the afternoon. Well,* she consoled herself, *at least I have a sitter arranged for tomorrow evening even if it had to be that Hannah Stillwaters girl. Better not be any more messes on the carpet like the last time.* "Salena? Where are you? Come here."

Sallie, the Singer of Songs, had literally been on cloud nine all week since her last meeting with Kenny the Koala Bear. Heavenly songs had permeated her mind and soul all week, and she had taken to writing them down in a little purple notebook that she kept hidden under the mattress so Horatio the Horrible wouldn't find them and rip them up. One was flowing through her now and she couldn't help but sing:

> *For He is the Father*
> *Of all that is Good*
> *He takes care of Everything*
> *That is understood*
> *He loves His children*
> *Both night and day*
> *Follow Him, trust Him and believe in Him*
> *He will lead the way.*

"Salena!!" Greedy Gertie's shrill voice broke into the beautiful melodic singing that had become her norm.

"Coming, momma." Salena ran down the hall to find Gertie with quite the scowl on her face. "Momma, do you want to hear my new song?"

"No, I do not. That infernal singing of yours is getting on my last nerve at the moment."

Undaunted, Sallie replied: "But, momma, I have to sing! I can't help it. It's like a bubbling brook inside of me that just has to spill out somewhere."

"Well, let it spill out somewhere else--preferably when I'm not around."

Sallie the Singer of Songs, refusing to let her spirit be dampened said as sweetly as possible, "What did you need, momma?"

Gertie was fussing with her hair as she sat at her vanity table. She turned to face Sallie now. "Just wanted you to know that tomorrow morning you will have to go with me to Horatio's clarinet lesson because Matilda is sick and won't be coming to clean tomorrow morning."

Now this grim news did cause Sallie the Singer of Songs' spirit to dampen and the smile left her lips and a slight frown came to her brow. If Matilda didn't come in the morning, she wouldn't be able to get up to the attic to see her beloved Kenny. There had to be some way she could stay home...but how? *Help me, my King,* she pleaded silently, *show me a way.*

Then, there it was: just like a sunbeam shining through a dark cloud, the answer came to her. "Momma, please, can I stay home if there is someone here to watch me? I really don't want to go to Horatio's clarinet lesson."

"There isn't anyone, Salena." Greedy Gertie refused to call Salena her new name, even though Sallie had asked her to. Sallie had been very careful to not disclose who gave her that name.

"Momma, since you have already asked Hannah to come tomorrow night, could she just come for the hour in the morning when you're at Horatio's lesson? It would be nice to have a girl to play with without Horatio around. Please, momma?"

"Oh, really, Salena, since when do you like Hannah so much. Seems like every time she comes over there is a problem. I just asked her to babysit when we go to the gala tomorrow night because no one else was available."

"Please, momma. I think if she comes over for awhile in the morning, I can make up for the last time she was here without Horatio butting in. Please--with pink sprinkles on top?"

Sallie's pleading was becoming wearisome to Gertie. "Oh, all right, let me call her mother and see if her mother says its o.k. As long as there are no more tea set episodes, understand?"

Sallie the Singer of Songs realized she had to set the record straight. "Momma, the tea set stains on the carpet, that wasn't Hannah's fault. I poured real tea into my tea set and Horatio pulled my hair when I was playing with my doll and then he kicked over the table and the tea set went flying and tea sprayed all over the rug. It happened before Hannah came over that day."

Greedy Gertie scowled at Sallie with a look of total disbelief. "Now don't blame Horatio for that. The real culprit is Hannah. I think you're covering for her. If I didn't have to have her here, I wouldn't. Now, enough of this talk."

"But, momma, it's the truth!"

"Truth, smoof. Truth is whatever we want it to be, Salena. You'll figure that out when you're all grown."

"Momma, I mean it. She didn't do it!"

"Salena, I understand that you're just a little girl and you just don't get it, but nonetheless, all this so-called "truth" talk is giving me a headache. If you want her here, fine. No need for stories. I'll call her mom and arrange it. Now, off with you--go play--I have important things to tend to." *Like making sure I am the most beautiful woman at the banquet tomorrow night,* she thought to herself.

Sallie the Singer of Songs felt a sadness overshadow her as she left her mother's bedroom. She comforted herself with the thought that maybe she could ask Kenny tomorrow morning why her mom could not stand to hear the truth. *Why would she want to cling to a lie when the truth was right in front of her?* What Sallie the Singer of Songs did not realize is that she had stumbled upon the very age old, perplexing question that confronts mankind down to this very date and time. One's eternal destiny is wrapped up in its answer.

Chapter Nineteen

The rugged sheriff had almost got his man when the phone rang at the Stillwaters' residence. It was Friday evening movie night in the den, with a bucket of good 'ole fried chicken and side fixings from a favorite local takeout brought home by Dad Stillwaters to give Judith a break from her daily cooking routine. The family had piled on top of stuffed pillows and a blanket on the soft rug to simulate a picnic, indoor style, complete with a small log fire in the fireplace that would be utilized for roasted marshmallows as an after dinner sweet treat. Daniel Stillwaters hit the pause button on the remote with a chicken greasy finger as Judith answered the call.

"Yes, no problem, just finishing dinner...tomorrow morning as well? Just an hour or so...no, she doesn't have any other plans. I'm sure she could use the extra money. All right, tomorrow at ten then. Good night."

Hannah looked quizzically at her mom. "Was that Gertie Pomposity again?"

"Yes. My, you have become the popular one with her of late! She wants you to babysit just Salena tomorrow morning when she takes Horatio to his clarinet lesson. It will only be for about an hour and, of course, it will add to the money you'll get from the evening sitting of both of the Pomposity children. One step closer to getting that oil painting set and artist easel, right?"

"Yes, indeed," smiled Hannah thinking dreamily on all the paintings she saw in her creative mind that longed for a canvas to express them upon. She had been saving for months, taking on extra chores around the house and the neighborhood in order to reach this longed-for goal. Her injured arm had put quite a damper on her pursuit of late, so, this unexpected babysitting, though a bit distasteful due to the nature and demeanor of the Pomposity house-hold in general and Greedy Gertie in particular, could very well turn out to be a blessing in disguise.

"Very well, pilgrim. Y'all ready to saddle up and head on back to the ranch?" Dad Stillwaters said in his best cowboy drawl.

"Yah, pawdner," giggled Hannah. Hit play, daddy do-right."

The Stillwaters settled cozily back into their home-on-the range movie where the good guys fought the bad guys in gun slinging style totally unaware of a more sinister battle raging on a far darker level than the wild west scene in play before them at this very moment.

Harry and Harvey Grungerider of the Smudge Pot clan in the Land of Mean were up to no good once again. It was Friday night and the dirty twins were finding no fun in their usual pranks of kick the full garbage can into the street scattering foul rotting trash everywhere or throwing rocks at passing cars and hightailing it behind thorny cactus barrels as shattering glass and screeching tires signaled a target had been reached. No, tonight felt different and their usual games just didn't bring the rank pleasure that destruc-tive actions generally brought to their darkened minds and souls. Something outside of themselves seemed to be goading them, sin-isterly directing them to new lows of depravity.

Harry drew in deeply on the lit cigarette in his fingers exhaling the foul smelling smoke into the still night air. Harvey took the last swig on the beer he had guzzled down in short order and with a flick of his wrist, sent the bottle flying over Harry's head, crashing into a thousand pieces several feet down the blackened asphalt road. He too felt the pull of evil from without tonight and was restless to do its bidding. "You up for a little adventure tonight, Harry?"

"Watcha got in mind?"

"How about giving that simpy do-good Ranger over in Pine Valley Forest a run for his money?"

Harry's mouth sported a twisted grin. "Sounds good to me."

"Let's hit it, then." The grungy twins hopped into an equally filthy beat-up junker of a car, spinning and squealing down the road as Harvey narrowly missed a car exiting its driveway, speeding off drag race car style towards Crystal Creek and beyond its borders to Pine Valley Forest. Hovering in flight close above this mechanical junk piece that was the teenage twins' mode of transportation, were the four evil emissaries of darkness, Hedgethorn, Prurient, Grimely and Odiferous, commissioned by their equally wicked commander, Nocturnicon, foul breath streaming as their cackling laughter permeated their dark night flight towards the peaceful forest.

It had been an early bed down for the Ranger this Friday evening. The daylight hours had kept him busy clearing fallen trees and brush from around the tower as well as helping with the planting of new pine saplings in a border area that had burnt out last year due to some careless campers whose unattended campfire had ended up burning 100 acres on the southern border of Pine Valley Forest. A cold sandwich supper and a micro waved cup of chicken soup were all that Rick the Red-Necked Ranger could manage before taking a steamy shower to wash off the day's grime before settling in bed with a novel that was taking him months to get through as only a few paragraphs in, and he was out like a light. Tonight was no different with the Ranger breathing heavily, night lamp still blazing, open book resting on his chest.

It was the first explosion that woke him from gentle slumber. It was the second and third that had him on his feet, grabbing his robe, and racing to his outdoor lookout that was his porch balcony via the sliding glass door. What he saw as he got there sent adrenaline coursing through his being. Yellow-orange flames of fire blazed in three different areas in the north campsite region of Pine Valley forest lighting up the otherwise dark horizon. Something within Rick the Red-Necked Ranger told him that this was no accident of some hapless camper. This was arson! The feel of evil was all about him and he felt chilled to the very bone. *Lord, help me, help my team,* he prayed as pants , boots and gear were yanked on in haste as he slid down the emergency pole from his tower home, sounding the ear-piercing alarm, signaling the forest troops and then speeding off pell mell in his small fire engine unit in the direction of the blaze. He knew it would be a long night and only the strength of his King could keep him awake and aware when weariness would inevitably take its toll. But, he knew as well, that a veritable army of fire trucks and men would soon arrive from Crystal Creek and beyond, fighting the fiery battle before them, backed as well by angelic unseen forces from on high.

Chapter Twenty

The morning sky was cloudy and overcast. "Watcha think, Puss Puss, are we going to have rain today?" Hannah nuzzled her face into the downy belly of her beloved feline as she stroked his head. Puss Puss B' Guss Guss had been perched on his kitty tree looking out at the day, but no sunshine was forthcoming in the window this morning to warm his fur. Fall weather was definitely settling in. As Hannah lifted her head to gaze out the window, Puss Puss B' Guss Guss jumped down from his kingly perch to place his bountiful body over the floor vent, warming his belly as the heater cycled on and off. "Oh, you just think you're in Maui on the beach, don't you?" cooed Hannah with one more chin scratch before she left the bedroom.

Hannah took a fleeting glimpse at her reflection in the hall mirror. She was a vision of pink today--hair tied back in a pony tail with a satin pink ribbon, long-sleeved, pink and white striped, soft-brushed cotton blouse, faded blue jeans, and neon pink and gray sneakers. *Yes, I do look the babysitting role. I sure hope this goes well this morning with Salena as I have to go back there tonight even if it doesn't*, she thought. She looked at the clock in the hall: 9:10. *Need to leave in about twenty minutes.* "Hey mom, do you think I'll need my heavy jacket this morning or just my light fleece?" Breakfast dishes were still stacked near the sink as Hannah came into the kitchen. "Mom?" Hannah went around the corner to the den and saw her mom and dad standing silently together, eyes transfixed on the television set. As she drew closer, the news lady's voice could be heard.

"Last night, a fire broke out in the northern section of Pine Valley forest. The blaze is still raging this morning and as of this moment, has not been brought under control. At this time, arson is definitely suspected as gasoline type explosions were heard by some campers near the area who fortunately were able to evacuate their campsite unharmed. Another person in the vicinity a few miles further north narrowly missed colliding with a vehicle simply described as "a junker" as it sped away from the direction of the fire. The witness indicated to official sources that they thought there were two people in the front seat of the vehicle, but were not completely sure because of the darkness. The Rangers are hard at work fighting this fire and units from surrounding areas have come in as back up early this morning. It is not clear as yet how much damage has been done or when this fire will be brought under control. We will bring you further updates as they become available. This is Renee Smith reporting for C-5 News. Back to you, Chet."

Judith and Daniel Stillwaters' faces looked grim as they turned from the set to notice Hannah in the room. "Mom, do you think Uncle Rick is all right?" Hannah felt sick to her stomach with the thought of anything bad happening to her favorite uncle.

Judith drew Hannah close, giving her a warm bear hug. Daniel came over and wrapped his arms around both his girls: the wonderful woman whose life and his had been intertwined for 20 years and the sweet flower of 11 that was his pride and joy. He softly answered Hannah. "We don't know, sweetheart. But we do know the One that does. Let's talk to Him about it and put all the cares and concerns in His more than capable hands." Knowing that wherever two or more are gathered together in His name, there He promises to be, this family of three knelt united in Him, by faith knowing that He heard.

"See you later this evening and remember, don't worry. Your Uncle Rick knows his stuff and he is in good hands. You spread some cheer to this home, o.k.?" Dad Stillwaters had given Hannah a ride to the Pomposities' home as he was heading back to the office to finish up a special task that needed to be done before Monday rolled around.

"O.k., dad, will do!" Hannah gave her dad a smile and a wave as she shut the car door and headed up the ornate stone walk that led to the Pomposities' front door. *Lord, please let this morning go quickly. I really can't handle a lot of upset.*

To her surprise, Sallie the Singer of Songs (but still known to Hannah as only Salena the Shrieker) opened the door before she had the chance to even ring the bell. "Hannah! I am so happy you came--come in."

The delightful demeanor of this pint-sized child quite took Hannah aback. In fact, it caused her to wonder if indeed she had come to the wrong house. Sallie, sensing Hannah's reticence, reached out and softly put her hand into Hannah's with Hannah following this little one's gentle leading down the hallway and into the kitchen. "How did you hurt your arm?" Before Hannah could go into that story, Salena excitedly said: "Momma is almost ready to go; would you like a doughnut? My daddy got them from the bakery this morning--they're really good!"

Sallie the Singer of Songs pushed the bakery box filled with doughnuts of all kinds--fruit filled, glazed, chocolate iced, pink with sprinkles, and the standard plain cake, good-for-dunking-in-milk-or-coffee doughnut. "Pick any one you want. The pink sprinkle ones are my favorite." Sallie set a small plate and napkin in front of Hannah. She settled on a cake doughnut with white icing and coconut mixed in. Sallie plopped down opposite Hannah on the kitchen stool with a pink sprinkle doughnut on her plate. Hannah took a bite, savoring the moist coconut and gooey vanilla icing on top of the melt-in-your mouth cake doughnut. Sallie bit daintily into her pink sprinkle iced doughnut and smiled at Hannah as she ate quietly. Hannah couldn't help but notice a light, a peace, yes, and downright joy in the eyes that met her gaze. This was a very different girl from the shrieking, screaming Salena of times so recent in memory. *I wonder what has happened.* So many thoughts, possibilities floated through her mind as she watched this young one. *Could it be?* But for now, all she felt at liberty to say as she once again found her voice for the first time since she had come through the door was, "Thank you, Salena. That is very thoughtful of you."

"You're welcome. Call me Sallie."

"Sallie?"

"Yes. I have a new name: Sallie the Singer of Songs." Sallie's voice quieted to a whisper causing Hannah to lean forward over the counter to hear. "A very special person gave me that name. I want you to meet him."

Before Hannah could ask who this friend was, the clacking of Greedy Gertie's high heels on the tile floor accompanied by the boisterous hollering of Horatio the Horrible shattered the peace of just moments before.

"Mom, she's eating another doughnut. That's not fair! I want another one too!"

"Stop it Horatio, we have to leave for your clarinet lesson. You can have another one when you get back!"

Horatio, not at all listening to Gertie, made a grab for the bakery box, which in turn, knocked into Hannah's plate sending doughnut and plate crashing to the floor.

"Oh, really, Horatio. Get into the car now!" With a sound thwack on his backside by Gertie, Horatio went running down the hall--the door out to the garage slamming seconds later.

Gertie, red faced with anger as well as embarrassment started to speak, but Hannah stopped her. "It's o.k., I'll get it cleaned up. You go on now. Sallie and I will be fine."

Greedy Gertie's face had started to soften at Hannah's words of reassurance, but then, her eyes flared with a meanness as she sputtered, "Her name is Salena. S - A - L - E - N - A. Salena. Do you understand? I don't want to hear that other ridiculous name, Sallie the Singer of Songs--singer of irritation, more than not. I'll be back in about an hour. Be good, SALENA!" Greedy Gertie drew the name out with a high shrill ending. And with that, Greedy Gertie Pomposity regained her cold-hearted composure, high heels clacking her departure, then muffled by the carpeted hallway. The slam of the garage door was double in volume of Horatio's.

Hannah braced herself, awaiting the ear piercing wails that were sure to soon emanate from Salena/Sallie while the resounding slam of the garage door still echoed in her ears. To her utter amazement, nothing of the sort transpired. Instead, a lilting melody broke the silence as Sallie the Singer of Songs brought forth a broom and dust pan from the corner kitchen closet and began to sweep up the shattered pieces of plate intermingled with Hannah's crumbled doughnut from the kitchen floor. Hannah held the dust pan as she stared at the joyful being before her, words as glistening as sun-lit diamonds with a voice as pure and clear as untouched mountain streams.

> *For His love is like a river*
> *Washing over me*
> *No dirt or stain of sin remains*
> *Because His Blood has set me free*
> *I used to be so sad and lonely*
> *Now I'm full of glee*
> *My King of Kings has come to stay*
> *Living in my heart right now*
> *And each and every day.*

As the last note of the song faded, Hannah dropped the dust pan and grabbed Sallie the Singer of Songs with her good arm, twirling her around and around, tears of joy and amazement flowing freely down her cheeks.

"Oh, Sallie, you know Him! You know Him! You truly do know Him!"

Hannah could not stop swirling and twirling Sallie about as she giggled back, "Yes, I do, I really do!"

Hannah's twirly whirly dance ended in the forbidden-to-children white living room where they plopped down on the couch, both too excited to even pay attention to their surroundings.

"When--where--how--who..." Hannah could only seem to utter mono-syllabic words as her euphoria at this great miraculous event of a transformed life before her made it hard to gather her thoughts into a cohesive, intelligible stream.

"That's what I wanted to tell you about, but I think it might be easier to show you while I have the chance to...but first," and at this Hannah noticed a sadness flit across the joyful eyes of this new creation wonder, "I want to tell you how sorry I am and ask you to forgive me."

"Forgive you? For what?"

"For the last time that you were here." Sallie brought her legs into a crossed leg position on the brocade cushioned couch facing Hannah. "Remember when I blamed you for the tea set mess in the living room here, and I told my mom that it was your fault when it wasn't and my mom yelled at you and said mean things to you and made you leave?"

"Yes, Sallie, I do, but it's o.k. You're little, and I'm not mad anymore."

"No, Hannah, it's not right. Not even if I am little. I knew it was a lie but I was scared of my mom and I never made it right; not until I met the King of Kings by asking Him to come into my heart and wash me clean. And then, I really knew it was very wrong. And I told my mom the truth the other day, but she didn't believe me--but I want you to know that I am really, really sorry and I told the King of Kings how sorry I was too. So, can you really forgive me now that you know the truth?"

Hannah felt such compassion surge through her at the transparency of this sweet, tender soul before her. "Yes, Sallie, Singer of beautiful songs! I truly forgive you. That is what we do when we belong to the King of Kings. He has forgiven us, made us His children, and when we mess up, we still go to Him and ask forgiveness and He will forgive us if we are truly sorry for what we have done. And then, we do just what you did. If we hurt someone, then we go to that person and ask them to forgive us. Remember: <u>He</u> is the only perfect one. He forgives us--we forgive others--and we tell others about Him so that forgiveness can set others free from their past and all the bad things they have done, and then they can have a new life, just like you do!"

Sallie the Singer of Songs breathed a big sigh of relief as she felt the forgiveness of her new friend in the Spirit wash over her, all anxiety gone, peace and joy restored. Giving Hannah a quick sisterly hug, she exclaimed, "Good, now I want to show you something truly wonderful. But hurry--before momma and Horatio get back."

And just like that, with jack rabbit speed, she was off racing from the living room down the hall to Horatio's room, to get the chair. Hannah, not quite as quick as this little spry bundle of energy, took a bit longer to get up off of the couch due to her one arm in a cast, and by the time she got to the hall, Sallie the Singer of Songs, chair in place, standing upon it tippy toe style, hit the button with showman like flair. She responded to Hannah's astonished "what are you up to?" look with a "tah-dah" spread of her arms as the attic stairs touched down upon the carpeted hallway.

"It's time to meet...*Kenny the Koala Bear!*" Without a backward glance, Sallie the Singer of Songs raced up the stairs with a puzzled Hannah following right at her heels.

Chapter Twenty-One

It had been a long night and from the look of things, was going to be a trying day as well. A soot covered, bone weary, Rick the Red-Necked Ranger slumped down on a tree trunk stump for a moment's rest from the battle against the raging inferno that had ripped through Pine Valley forest overnight. It seemed that each time they made a bit of headway in containing the fire on one front, the wind would pick up setting new timber ablaze on another front. Discouragement had settled over many of the Rangers and fire crew that had come in mass from several communities adjoining Crystal Creek. All forces had been battling virtually shoulder to shoulder throughout the long night into the late morning hours. Sandwiches and vitamin water had been gathered and brought to the scene by the kind folk in Crystal Creek who had rallied the community into action and sent them out to the forest line via Angel of Mercy Vans, an official agency that worked with fire and rescue teams in times of crisis.

"You look like you could use one of these." Rick, head in hands, gazed up at a fellow Ranger, holding out a ham and cheese sandwich in sooty hands. Rick managed a half smile. "Thanks, brother." Rick took a bite, realizing how famished he actually was and polished off the sandwich in no time. "There's more where that came from--over there." A long folding table had been set up outside of the Angel of Mercy vans, piled high with sandwiches, chips, water, cookies, oranges and apples. As Rick headed to get another sandwich, his fellow Ranger hollered after him, "Hey--bring me a couple of waters back."

"No problem," replied the weary Ranger. As he perused the goodies on the table before him, grabbing a bit of everything, the young volunteer behind the table smiled kindly. "Take as much as you want--there's plenty. And by the way, you guys are doing a terrific job. Please know that we're all praying for you too."

As Rick made his way back to his fellow fire fighters, he reflected a bit. *Prayer. That was certainly needed right now.* It had felt like they were battling the very fires of hell all night. There was just something so wicked afoot. Ungodly. Definitely the presence of evil and unseemly dark forces involved here. The Ranger had fought many a fire in his day, but this one just felt different. This was purposeful. Planned. With an intent not only to destroy, but to distract.

Distract? Distract him from something. Something important. Something about to take place that would require his strength and attention that now was being literally drained from his very being. As the Ranger drew near to where his fellow comrades in the fire fight awaited him for more physical refreshment, Rick the Red-Necked Ranger knew what he must do before going back to the fire battle. He put his fingers in his cheeks, giving his characteristic loud Ranger whistle. Several battle weary heads of the crew taking a needed respite from the flames turned his way. Rick wasted no time. "Gather around, men." The authority in his voice drew the fatigued men to his side. Gazing around at the charcoaled faces, the Ranger boldly proclaimed: "We need to pray."

The emissaries of darkness hovered in flight above the black and grey smoke intermingled with orange searing flames spreading through the deep, dense forest floor. "It's so easy to get those humans to do our bidding," cackled Grimely. "Did you see those gasoline can explosions set by our daring duo?" Prurient was referring to Harry and Harvey Grungerider who had thoroughly enjoyed filling the three empty gasoline cans from their trunk at the all night convenience store, complete with the purchase of another six-pack of beer with their fake i.d. The setting aflame of the containers and ensuing explosions had been the highlight thrill to date for the delinquent twins. The near miss of their car as Harry drunkenly weaved and sped out of the north woods campsite added to the raw nerve, dark deed adrenaline rush.

"Yeah, those twits almost got caught," hissed Spearnobus.

"But they didn't," chimed in Hedgethorn. "The boss ought to be pleased with our inspired handiwork. Hope it burns the whole forest down. Maybe the whole town--wouldn't that be grand!" The distastefully evil chorus of laughter filled the air high above the beautiful forest that was being savagely ravaged by the flames below.

Unbeknownst to these demons of darkness who had been proudly ogling the destruction beneath them, they missed viewing what was taking place directly above their ugly heads. Large, ominous, moisture dense clouds were rapidly forming, soon to carry answers to the prayer warriors below. The bone weary men had gained renewed strength in their spirits after their round of intense prayer before the King of Kings. And...this answer would come in liquid form. Rain was on its way!

Nothing on earth could have adequately prepared Hannah for what awaited her in the musty attic world that had become a place of refuge and spiritual sustenance to Sallie the Singer of Songs via her Saturday morning rendezvous with her chocolate furred mentor and compadre. It took a few moments for Hannah's eyes to adjust to the dimly lit box, trunk and bag littered space as Sallie flicked on the lights, then flitted graceful as a ballerina far across the attic to a space beneath a small, dust-encrusted window. Pausing in front of a trunk, she bid Hannah in earnest, "Quickly, he's in here." Kneeling on the dusty wood-worn floor, with her perplexed babysitter Hannah at her side now, Sallie fished deep within her jean front pocket and brought forth the most unusual key that Hannah had ever seen.

As Sallie deftly put the filigreed key into the antique trunk's keyhole, she gave a quick glance at Hannah. "Get ready." The loud click of the key turning gave Hannah a bit of a start in the otherwise quiet hush of anticipation that enveloped her. Sallie slowly opened the intricately carved, dark cedar lid and Hannah peered inside. On top of a beautiful, but aged, multi-colored quilt, rested a fluffy, chocolate brown bear.

"Ohhhh...what a sweet looking bear. Is this what you wanted me to see?" As Hannah reached out to touch him, Kenny the Koala Bear opened his eyes.

"Well, hello there. And who might you be?"

Hannah let out a shriek that probably reached the decibel levels of the former Salena the Shrieker days. She backed away so quickly that she knocked over several lightweight boxes that went careening to the dusty floor.

"It's o.k., it's o.k, don't be scared," reassured Sallie. "This is my friend, Kenny the Koala Bear. He won't hurt you." Hannah had continued to back away from both Sallie and the strange trunk discovery. As she stared in amazement from across the room, Kenny hopped out of the trunk and landed a few feet away from Sallie.

"What on earth?! Sallie, where's the remote control? Quit scaring me like that! Come on now." Hannah felt like quite the silly fool for hollering and reacting to a toy koala bear. Yet, he really <u>did</u> look like the genuine article. Dusting herself off from the dirt shower she got when she banged into the boxes, she began to walk back towards Sallie. "Show me how he works so I can make him walk and talk too, Sallie."

"He's not a toy, Hannah. He's alive. Just like you and me."

Hannah, now in front of Sallie, got down on her haunches to get at eye level with her. "Sallie, it's fine if you want to play an imaginary game with your toys and pretend they can walk and talk or have a remote control toy that does do those things, but, sweetie, now that you belong to the King of Kings you can't lie and say something is alive when it's just a toy. If you're playing a game with me, just say so and I will play too. And, we'll have lots of fun together, o.k.?"

Due to Hannah's intense focus on Sallie with her fervent attempt to make her understand the seriousness of truth vs. lie, fiction vs. fact, etc., she failed to see the slow advance of Kenny the Koala Bear behind her. The touch of soft fur on the side of her face caused her to whirl around, eye to eye with Kenny the Koala Bear as he spoke so softly, yet clearly: "She's not lying Hannah. Just like you belong to the King of Kings, she does too and she told you the truth. I am alive!" Looking at those eyes only inches from her own affirmed to her the unbelievable, incomprehensible, though absolutely unmistakable truth. However it was possible, this bear was indeed, alive!

Totally overwhelmed by this irrefutable revelation, Hannah grabbed at an old, stuffing come loose pillow near her foot and sank down onto it. At a complete and utter loss for words, she continued to stare at the bear as he sat down as well, opposite her and next to Sallie who patted his fur. Finally, Hannah managed a weak, "how...?" but couldn't finish her thought.

The Koala did it for her. "Hannah, with the King of Kings all things are possible. We don't have much time this morning, but just hear these few things. He has sent me here on a mission. One that has just begun with this little one. Before knowing Him, she was Salena the Shrieker. Now, His Grace has transformed her into Sallie the Singer of Songs. I am soon to leave here, but the King's work will continue."

The look of amazement on Hannah's face made the bear smile. "And you will have a great part to play in that work as well, Hannah. The King has told me so."

"How can I hear and understand your speech--you're a bear!"

"That is a mystery you will have to take up with the King of Kings. But, one thing I can tell you--those who are in darkness cannot see the light unless their eyes and ears are opened by Him. You are in His Kingdom and so now is young Sallie."

"Is that why momma and daddy and Horatio think you're just a stuffed bear--because they're still in the Kingdom of Darkness?" Sallie asked.

"The simplest way I can explain that is that those who have the life of the King within them can see things that pertain to life and godliness and those who don't, see things as lifeless. Our King is life and truth and when we are in Him, we see things as they truly are--with the eye of the Spirit, not with our natural eyes. In other words, He causes us to see the truth about everything--not just how it seems to appear."

Hannah was just about to ask another question of this phenomenal bear when Sallie jolted upright. "They're back, Hannah! I hear the garage door closing--hurry!"

Kenny, with a bound and a hop, was back in the trunk and as the two were peering down at him before the inevitable closing of the lid, the gentle koala bear, looking directly at these two children of the King, said, "Your answer is in these words from our King: *"... Except a man be born again, he cannot see the kingdom of God."* (John 3:3). The girls softly closed the trunk and then ran like Olympic sprinters, flipping off the light switch and nearly tumbling down the stairs. Salena hit the button to retract them back into the ceiling above, and Hannah, one handed, pell melled the chair down the hall from whence it came. They barely made it into Sallie's room, flouncing on the bed amidst the pile of dolls and stuffed animals as the inner door from the garage to the house banged open. The chaotic presence of Horatio the Horrible and Greedy Gertie had returned, darkness careening into light.

Chapter Twenty-Two

The walk home from the Pomposity home was a blur. Hannah was so lost in thought over what had transpired in the Pomposity attic that she didn't seem to set her feet back into her known reality until she was once again walking up the familiar path that led to her door. A glance at the driveway told her that mom must be out on some errands and she knew that dad wouldn't be back until evening. She reached in her pocket for the very ordinary door key and she paused, turning it over in her hands, her thoughts returning back to the attic and the intricate, old-fashioned key that Salena, *I mean, Sallie,* had used to unlock that antique wood trunk that was home to...*a talking koala bear?* Hannah shook her head as if to try and wake herself--*was she in a dream?* She inserted the key in the run-of-the mill, standard door lock, and entered into the warmth that was her world. A home of peace and joy and love and...*meowr?* The white fluff bundle that was her confidante, had come bounding into the room, leaving the kitty tree of her room, awakened from his nap by the sound of human arrival.

"Oh, Puss Puss. Glad to see you too, Mr. meow bucket." Hannah picked up the purring bundle of feline love, and burrowed her face in his soft as silk fur carrying him into the kitchen for a kitty treat. On the counter was a note from mom: "Will be back around 2:00--gone to help make sandwiches for the Angel of Mercy people to take to the fire fighters. There are some sandwiches in the fridge for you too--love you."

Hannah plopped Puss Puss B' Guss Guss down next to his kitty bowl and opened the lower cabinets next to it. Shaking a bag of salmon treats to get his attention, and getting the sniff approval as she opened it, Hannah shook out a few tasty morsels into his bowl. "There you go, Puss Puss."

Besides the unreality of everything that had taken place this morning, Hannah kept sensing that there was something about this morning's encounter that had relation to something else--some other connection--some other time. *What was it?* Hannah left Puss Puss B' Guss Guss to his merry munching and wandered deep in thought into the family den. The room was done in rustic western, so fitting for the movie watched..*was it just last night...seems like eons ago. What's wrong with me?* It was as though past and present were a jumble--time had lost definition somehow.

Hannah flounced onto the leather couch that looked like something from a western ranch house. She stretched out, absently gazing across the room at the grizzled gunfighter clock and antique brass candelabras that could have been part of an old west hotel decor from the 40's. *A bear that quotes scriptures...a little brat turned beautiful...songs about the King...a new name for Salena...names...what kind of bear did she say...?*

Without warning, the flood gates opened. No barrier between past and present now. The recesses of her memory swung open wide to the scene in the woods. It now played forth in dramatic color before her mind's eye as though she were watching it on the blank television screen directly in front of her. Dogs barking--hundreds of them gathered together. Rick the Red-Necked Ranger was there, seeming to be in communication of some sort with them. A glimpse of what looked like Puss Puss B' Guss Guss in a knapsack strapped to the back of a golden retriever--and--before the horrible breaking sound of the tree branch that had plummeted her to the forest floor below, followed by her screams...followed by darkness...she recollected the voice of her Uncle Rick shouting: "You are now commissioned--onward to rescue *Kenny the Koala Bear!*"

Hannah sat bolt upright. This was like a dream--except that it wasn't. Hannah's hand went to her mouth, like a shock response, thoughts racing rapid fire in every direction. She sprang to her feet, and began to pace--back and forth in front of the couch. "It's real... it's real...all of it...all of it..." The puzzle pieces, so elusive until now, were coming together, forming a cohesive unit, a real true picture instead of just a jumble of disjointed bits of color and varying shapes in a puzzle box. As she paced, she began to speak aloud--to no one at all--except for the Puss Puss, his hunger momentarily tamed until next feed and looking for lovings from his favorite human.

"It actually happened...the dogs...the woods...Uncle Rick...telling them to go rescue a bear...a koala bear named Kenny..the bear I met... *today?!*" Puss Puss B' Guss Guss rubbed against his master's legs and did his flopsker routine onto the braided rug--belly wide open--looking for skritching. Hannah noticed her sweet pet looking so expectantly up at her. She obeyed--a well trained human--wrapped around all four of his paws.

"Oh, Puss Puss! I wish you could talk. You were there in those woods, weren't you?" "But, how is that even possible?" All that greeted the ears of the expectant Hannah were rumbling purrs. "I really <u>have</u> lost it Puss Puss! Now I expect you to talk too. Just like that koala bear did today over at the Pomposity house. I can't tell momma and daddy about this, Puss Puss. I remember the last time. They will think I have gone bonkers for sure. Oh, Puss Puss. What do I do? I have to tell someone."

And the only someone I can tell would have to be...Uncle Rick. Hannah looked at the old west clock. The hands pointed straight up to 12 o'clock noon. High noon. Time for a show down. Time for all the pieces to be glued together. Hannah hammed up her best gunfighter mimicked ramble into the kitchen, picked up the receiver from the land line phone, punching in the numbers to her Uncle Rick's Ranger tower home.

Light pin drops of moisture began to grace the Ranger's face as the other rangers and firefighters from surrounding communities resumed their battle against the raging inferno that engulfed Pine Valley forest's north section. Rick went forth refreshed on the wings of a supernatural, heaven-sent strength that sent new vigor into his bone weary body due to the fervent joint prayers of his fellow men just moments before. He sensed a break in the stranglehold that the powers of darkness had fiercely held since the fire first broke out last night. Hope was once more springing up from deep inside his innermost being. And, *could it be...?* The pin drops were now becoming splashes of raindrops on his cheeks. Rick the Red-Necked Ranger gazed upward for the first time noticing the dense clouds rolling in, a thick dark blanket in the sky descending low over the forest.

Boom! The clap of thunder gave him a jolt and the heavens let loose in the next instant. A torrential downpour began, quickly and powerfully turning into literal sheets of rain. "Praise God, praise God, praise God! Hallelujah!" Rick threw his fire hat in the air, doing a little happy jig, reminiscent of childhood. "Thank you Lord!" The grateful Ranger dropped to his knees, arms raised to the heavens in total abandonment and thanksgiving to the King of Kings.

The phone rang for what seemed like an eternity. Then, the familiar male voice came from the answering machine: "Hey, sorry I missed your call--probably out on forest patrol. Leave a message and I'll get back with ya." Hannah could have kicked herself. *What was I thinking? Of course he's not home. He's out fighting the forest fire. Now what? How can I explain all of this in a quick message?* All these musings raced through Hannah's mind before the inevitable "beep" sounded.

"Umm...hi, Uncle Rick, this is Hannah...umm...hope you're o.k. I have something I really need to talk to you about. It's about a bear named Kenny--I met him this morning. I'm going back to the house where he's at tonight around 5:00 to babysit the kids that live there. Ummm...please call back as soon as you can. I have a lot of questions..." *beep.* The machine cut off. Hannah slowly put the phone back on its hook. "Now what, Puss Puss?" Hannah bent down to give her fluffy friend a few more pets as he rubbed against her legs.

Chapter Twenty Three

A thoroughly drenched, muddy, beyond tired Ranger ascended his tower home. The Heaven-sent rain had done its job and the raging inferno gave way to smoldering embers that soon died out. The skeleton crew remained just to make sure that nothing was left to re-start a blaze. It was 5:00 now. The Ranger left his muddy gear in the entry way and headed for the shower. The hot water and soap suds were a balm to his body as well as to his soul. Was it tonight that Bubba and the special team would be by for an update on Kenny? Maybe just a brief nap. The exhausted, battle weary Ranger collapsed on his bed, failing to notice the blinking red light of his answering machine before slumber overtook him.

The Special Forces team with Sergeant Bubba Doo Wah Wah at its helm, had met with disappointment after disappointment in the weeks since Kenny the Koala Bear had gone missing. In fact, not even an inkling of a possibility to his whereabouts or a fine hair of a clue had turned up in either the Crystal Creek area, Pine Valley Forest, the Land of Mean or any outlying rural areas or communities surrounding them. It was as if the Bear had literally vanished. Bubba absolutely refused to fear the worse despite the futile high and low searches, the meetings after long days and nights, grim-faced recruits that bore not an ounce of positive news. And that's what he had to deliver to his favorite ranger at their meeting that would take place tonight. A big pile of nothing.

And then there were the almost daily calls from a heartbroken Katie Koala. Though her faith remained strong, he could still sense the pain of a momma's heart, longing to see the face of her cub again, to know everything was o.k., simply to know that he was safe. *There just had to be a breakthrough in this case. Kenny just can't be gone. Maybe after the meeting with the Ranger, I can make it back to Crystal Creek to see if that pampered Puss Puss B' Guss Guss has gleaned anything from the feline community.* To date, that had proved an empty source of info as well.

"Ready to go Sarge?" Lance Corporal James the beagle and Corporal Gerald the German shepherd looked expectantly at their canine leader. This team had of late been scouring the Pine Valley forest area together with the Koala team for the past several days before the fire broke out.

"2000 on the dot. Let's go men."

The Ranger tower was dark. Only the outside high post light lit the Special Forces' way as they padded down the path. "The Ranger must be asleep. Probably collapsed from the fire fight," growled Corporal Gerald, the German shepherd.

"You know what to do then, team." Bubba Doo Wah Wah reared up, front paws on the rugged light pole craftily made by the Ranger from a fallen tree trunk. Straining his strong neck, he took ahold of the knot in the long sisal rope that sported a very large iron bell suspended high above their heads located adjacent to the Ranger's bedroom window. As the bell swung to and fro at each firm pull of Bubba's strong jowls, sending forth a deep resonant *clang...clang...*

clang... Corporal Gerald and Lance Corporal James sent forth a baleful wailing: "*awooo...awoo...awoo...*", quite the cacophony of sound that not even the soundest of sleepers would be able to continue onward in restful slumber.

Sure enough, a bleary-eyed, tussled hair Ranger staggered out onto the porch landing, coming to a halt at the railing, peering down at the canines semi-shrouded in the darkness below.

"Sergeant Bubba Doo Wah Wah and Special Commissioned Forces reporting as requested, Senior Ranger Sir."

The Ranger groggily responded: "Good evening, gentlemen. Please excuse my appearance. Come up the back stairs and let yourselves in. I will be with you momentarily." The Ranger left the porch, returning to his inner tower home in order to ready himself.

Rick splashed water on his face, washing the sleep from his eyes. He ran a quick comb through his hair, slicking it down with his wet hands. Tucking his shirt back into his pants, he sat down on the chair in the main area, pulling on his boots in short order. *8:00 p.m.?! Must have forgotten to set the alarm.*

Just as the canines were coming through the door, which had been left slightly ajar for them, the Ranger's eye caught the blinking red answering machine light on the table beside him. "Just a moment, gentlemen. Let me check this message first."

The faithful trio, Sergeant Bubba Doo Wah Wah, Corporal Gerald the German shepherd and Lance Corporal, James the beagle, never got to relay the unsuccessfulness of their search thus far. But the shock and delight of the look on the canines' faces as well as Rick the Red-Necked Ranger would definitely have been one to capture for time and eternity when the voice of the Ranger's niece, Hannah, said the immortal words, "*it's about a bear named Kenny--I met him this morning...*"

Chapter Twenty-Four

I t didn't take long for Horatio the Horrible to be in his usual fine form of horrid behavior for the evening. Hannah had arrived promptly at 5:00 to be greeted by an elegantly clad Greedy Gertie and Pugnacious Pomposity, III swiftly ushering her in, instructions quickly given by Gertie for bedtime snacks, etc., with Pugnacious palming a $20 bill for the pizza delivery that would be arriving around 5:30.

The Pomposities had then sailed out the door with the expected "Be good, children" with a particular glare at Horatio by Gertie and then Hannah was left to her own devices of maintaining order betwixt the Pomposity children. With Salena the Shrieker now miraculously changed into Sallie the Singer of Songs, Hannah knew that on this front, at least, there would be no problems. With the arrival of the large pepperoni pizza, all attention was given to feeding hungry appetites and doling out second rounds of soda and brownies for dessert--all served on paper plates and disposable cups at the kitchen counter.

The problem began shortly after 6:00. With the kitchen easily put back into order, Hannah and her charges headed to the Pomposity family room to select a movie for the evening's entertainment. Hannah had forgotten to bring a movie that would have solved the ultimate problem of choosing, but, with the early morning's events still swimming in her mind, she had left it on the counter at home. Sallie quickly chose a family adventure movie about rambunctious raccoons that disrupt a family's weekend camp-out. Horatio jumped up from the couch and knocked the case out of her hands before she could even open it.

"Horatio, don't do that," implored Hannah. We can take turns watching a movie. Let's watch this one first and then we can watch one that you want to watch."

"We've seen that stupid movie a zillion times," retorted Horatio. "And, I'm sick of it." Bending down in front of the DVD bookcase next to the large television screen, Horatio grabbed a sci-fi adventure and proceeded to go for the remote control. Hannah intercepted him. "No, Horatio," she firmly asserted, "we don't behave like that. We will take turns. You don't knock a movie out of your sister's hands to get your way."

Horatio had a look of hatred in his eyes that was particularly unnerving as he faced Hannah. "Fine, then--have it your way." He sent the DVD flying across the family room, narrowly missing Sallie. Before Hannah could get ahold of him, he fled the room, hollering as he ran down the hallway, "I'd rather be in my room anyway and play my video games than be with two stupid, ugly girls." The bedroom door slammed and the click of the lock followed.

Hannah was about to go after him, but Sallie stopped her. "It's better to let him be when he's like this. He'll be all right. He won't break anything in his room, that's for sure. Come on, Hannah. Let's watch the movie." Hannah popped the DVD into the player and the two settled into the very comfortable, brown suede couch. As the movie began, Sallie snuggled close to Hannah and in a whisper said, "Maybe in a couple of hours, Horatio will fall asleep. He got up really early this morning because he was out looking for night crawlers so that he and dad can go fishing tomorrow. If he falls asleep, we can go see Kenny before momma and daddy come home, o.k.?" Hannah returned the smile that now came so readily to Sallie's face, and nodded her head. Little did she realize what a night it would truly turn out to be.

Greedy Gertie was definitely in her element as she waltzed about the ballroom, diamond necklace radiantly glistening, catching every ray of light from the numerous crystal chandeliers that hung majestically over the dance floor. Her black silk, floor-length gown swirled elegantly about her as Pugnacious Pomposity, III glided her across the floor in perfect three step, waltz rhythm as the live orchestra music played. A mink and ermine stole was lightly draped across her otherwise bare shoulders. Pugnacious, in his jet black tuxedo and tails, white starched French cuff shirt, perfectly complimented Gertie's ensemble. The dinner had been perfect as well: prime rib *au jus*, new potatoes, candied baby carrots, fresh from the oven sourdough rolls, and New York cheesecake topped with fresh strawberries and a mint garnish.

"Isn't this a wonderful evening, Pugnacious! We are the talk of the ball. Several of the ladies from the country club were positively drooling over the new necklace you bought me. And your speech--the thunderous applause. We have absolutely climbed to a much higher rung on the social elite ladder tonight."

"Most definitively, my dear," replied Pugnacious Pomposity, III, delusions of grandeur and recognition swelling his mind, causing him to raise his nose ever so slightly higher into the air as he peered down at what he deemed as unfortunate mortals swishing about the dance floor. *Poor fools, he mused, none of you will ever be able to climb to the heights I have reached this evening.*

It was less than a split second's worth of silence as the machine message came to an end, rapidly replaced by shouts and ooh-rahs with canine forces and the Ranger losing all sense of decorum and dignity. Hugs and paw-5's, hooting, hollering, barking, foot stomping, paws prancing. It was quite the scene of exuberance! The Ranger was the first to regain his composure. "I just can't believe it. How in the world did my little niece find out where Kenny is. All of our forces--for weeks, and she finds him--unbelievable!"

Bubba Doo Wah Wah could barely contain himself as he started for the door. "What are we waiting for? Let's go get him!"

"Whoa--hang on there, my good canine friend, let's play the message again to find out what house she's at." Thus began a series of three replays with the frustrating realization that Hannah had not given the location of the house she was babysitting at this evening- -just that Kenny was at *that* house, wherever that elusive house was located. The four paused, deep in thought as to the next step to take.

Bubba was the first to venture a suggestion. "Sr. Ranger, Sir--it might be a long shot, but if we could get over to Hannah's house, I could, under this cover of nightfall, rally the Puss Puss B' Guss Guss and see if perhaps he knows Hannah's whereabouts for the evening. He is her confidante after all--her pal--her pet. He must have over- heard some clue from his human."

"I believe you've hit the proverbial nail right on the head, Sgt. Doo Wah Wah." Formality had returned to the Special Forces and the Ranger in charge as was their custom when on a mission. "And time's a wasting--to the truck men! It'll take us a good hour to get there. We've got a bear long overdue for rescue!"

Hannah and Sallie let out a joint giggle as the climactic silly esca- pade of the raccoon family brought the film's finale. As the screen credits rolled, Sallie left Hannah's side and skipped into the kitchen. The clanking and clattering of utensils being rummaged through soon followed. "Watcha doing, Sallie?" Hannah had followed her small charge who was tearing through a medium-sized drawer in the kitchen cabinet.

"I'm looking for a special screwdriver. It's small and long and... ahhh--here it is!"

"Why do you need a screwdriver?"

Sallie smiled and motioned very dramatically in a "come follow me" gesture and Hannah obliged, Sallie leading the way down the carpeted hallway, stopping in front of Horatio's door. No light came forth from under the door and no sounds issued from behind the locked door either. Whispering, Sallie said, "I've watched mom and dad use this screwdriver to open his door when he locks himself in. We have to make sure he's asleep; otherwise, he'll follow us up into the attic and cause all kinds of problems."

Deftly, young Sallie inserted the long, thin screwdriver with the red handled end, and sure enough, a tiny turn and a soft click was heard. Sallie slowly turned the knob and pushed the door open. The only light in the dark room came from a distant outlet where a blue action hero nightlight burned. As their eyes adjusted to the dim room, they could make out the outline of Horatio the Horrible, sound asleep on his bed. Sallie carefully grasped the desk chair that would be needed to reach the staircase button, and Hannah kept the door open wide as Sallie slowly maneuvered the chair through the door. As it cleared the door frame, Hannah gently pulled the door closed behind her so that Horatio would not be awakened. In her haste to exit the room, the door was not fully latched at her too gentle closure. As she and Sallie excitedly made their way up the attic stairs, the door came loose from the latch and swung halfway open.

Chapter Twenty-Five

The air of anticipation was electrifying as the Ranger, driving as fast as legally possible on the winding two-lane highway, commandeered their journey from Pine Valley Forest to Crystal Creek. Bubba Doo Wah Wah kept seeing in his mind's eye the excitement, joy and relief that was soon to come to Katie Koala when he would bring the long-lost bear home to her loving motherly arms. If not for the darkness of the night as well as the intensity of their collective focus, they otherwise might have noticed the break in the guard railing at that long last bend in the road where an out-of-control "junker" vehicle had plummeted through just the night before. The wreckage was swift after its sheer descent into the depths of the ravine far below. Two young lives who had lived in recklessness and wickedness had met their sad, tragic end. They were now beyond any hope of turning their lives around and being in the Kingdom of Light. Instead, they would remain trapped in the clutches of the hater of their souls in eternal torment in the Kingdom of Darkness forever.

Whether it was the call of nature from too many sodas before bed, the distracting hall light streaming into his room or the sound of ringing in the distance, or possibly, the combination of all three,

Horatio the Horrible stumbled out of bed, and picked up the hall phone from its cradle.

"Hello?" he mumbled sleepily.

"Horatio--what are you doing up? Hasn't Hannah put you children to bed yet?" Greedy Gertie fumed into the phone.

"Uhh, no, uhhh...I fell asleep. Just got up to go to the bathroom..."

"Well, where is Hannah? Put her on the phone."

Horatio, for the first time since arousing from his slumbered stupor, glanced down the hallway. What he saw there made him angry. And jealous. And with a desire for revenge. The chair. Beneath the button to open the attic staircase. And the staircase was withdrawn into the ceiling.

"Well, that might take a bit of time, momma. You see, they aren't down here with me right now."

"What are you talking about Horatio. For heavens' sake--make some sense! What do you mean "not down with you"? Where is Hannah?"

"They, Hannah and Salena, are up in the attic."

"The attic!" screamed Gertie so loudly that Pugnacious motioned to her to quiet down as some fellow gala attendants had turned in their direction to see what all the fuss was about.

"Yes, momma--the attic. You remember that key that you were looking for a few weeks ago. Well, Salena found it and we went up into the attic and found out that it fit a trunk--and we opened it and saw the koala bear in there that you brought home and..."

The shrill shriek that emanated from Greedy Gertie almost made Horatio the Horrible drop the phone and caused more than a few irritated stares to come from the ballroom party guests, so much so that Pugnacious ushered Gertie quickly out a side door onto a garden patio to avoid further embarrassment from her uncontrollable outbursts of rage when riled.

"You listen to me, Horatio and listen good! We will be home before you can say "horse feathers"--trust me on that account! Now, here is what I want you to do and you follow my directions to the letter or it will be your hide, do you understand?"

"Yes, mom...o.k...., ok......will do." And with an evil gleam anticipating the upcoming fireworks soon to transpire, Horatio the Horrible quietly set the phone on the cradle and began to execute his part in the plan.

It was just past 9:00 when the canine trio and the Ranger arrived in the Stillwaters' neighborhood. The Ranger quietly glided the truck into a cul-de-sac about four blocks from Hannah's parents' home in front of a vacant lot that contained several overhanging willow trees that he parked beneath in order to avoid attention. "It's all on your shoulders now, my friend." The Ranger had gotten out of the car and walked a ways from the vehicle so that he could talk to Bubba Doo Wah Wah alone. He bent down and gave his partner an affectionate pat. "And, no better shoulders could there be to rest upon--go get that Puss Puss to fess up to what he knows!" As Bubba bounded away, the Ranger quietly said, "And I pray he does know where Kenny is," as he turned on his heel returning to the truck where now all they could do was wait.

Bubba Doo Wah Wah was in high form tonight. As he wove from cover to cover, a bush here, hidden behind a trash can there, his military training caused him to be that stealthy warrior bent on securing the facts that would complete the "K Mission" given weeks ago by General Sedmeyer for the safe return of Kenny the Koala Bear. Approaching headlights on the street caused Bubba to swiftly take cover in the long row of privet bushes. One more block and he would be at his destination, the Stillwaters' home. Puss Puss B' Guss

Guss had been of no help at their last meeting. *He just has to know something tonight--he just has to!*

The coast now clear as the car streamed past in the street, Bubba Doo Wah Wah now loped across the lawns in long strides. Up ahead he could see the light from Hannah's room, casting a soft glow. *Hopefully, the Puss Puss will be in his usual spot on the kitty tree awaiting his human's return home.* Spying the van in the driveway alerted Bubba that the adult Stillwaters were more than likely inside. This would take a bit of finesse. No loud barking or they would be roused to his presence. Bubba silently positioned himself beneath Hannah's window. Rearing up onto his hind legs, he placed his paws on the brick ledge. With one paw, he lightly tapped his claws on the window. He did the standard signal, well known to Puss Puss B' Guss Guss. Three taps and a pause. Three taps and a pause. Three taps and a pause. But this time instead of the typical two loud barks, he muted them to two soft barks. He repeated the sequence once more, and hid himself in the bushes.

Bubba waited...and waited...and waited. No ruffle of the curtains. No responding mew. Exasperated with nerves on edge, Bubba Doo Wah Wah muttered to himself, "Of all nights for Puss Puss B' Guss Guss to not respond--is he being dense or what?" Once more Bubba resumed his hind quarter position, and instead of the muted barks, took the chance of discovery and gave the two loud barks in the right sequence. Just as he feared, the Stillwaters front door opened with Bubba diving for cover beneath the bushes, narrowly avoiding discovery. As broken bush branches dug into his coat, Bubba growled, "Drat that Puss Puss! This is going to cost him some fur, for sure." Before he could rant further, the familiar form of the persnickety fluffy feline suddenly appeared in the window frame. Waiting until he heard the solid click of the front door closing, Bubba Doo Wah Wah ventured forth, greatly relieved when he gazed up and saw the nonplussed fluff ball peering down at him. He returned the disinterested look with a glare that Puss Puss B' Guss Guss was quite familiar with--a look that said: *if we weren't on the same team, you would be fluff in my dog bowl!*

Bubba watched as Puss Puss quickly entered the spring loaded, hidden door in the kitty tree, making his way down its interior space and then the *meowr* inside the planter wine barrel and out on the sidewalk he pranced to gaze up at the edgy, miffed Bubba.

"What's got you so stirred up tonight, drool jowls?"

"I don't have time for your insults, Puss Puss. You nearly got me caught! I thought you felines had better hearing than that!"

"Oh, I heard you the first time. It's just you caught me during bath time and I had a stubborn toenail that needed to come loose."

"Puss Puss, one day..."

"Oh, one day what, Bubba? You're all bark and no bite." The Puss Puss pranced in and out of the four legs of Bubba as they bantered back and forth. "Anyway, why are you here? This is definitely an unscheduled meeting and the night air is a bit chill."

"Puss Puss," glowered Bubba. "This is very, very serious. The Ranger and the Special Canine Forces are awaiting me a few blocks from here. Your human, Hannah, left a message on the Ranger's answering machine earlier today saying that she had met Kenny the Koala Bear and..."

"Yah--know all about it--yesterday's news." Puss Puss B' Guss Guss lazily flopped down and began to lick his front paw.

It took every bit of self control within Bubba Doo Wah Wah to refrain from grabbing the feline by the scruff of the neck and giving him a good shake. "Listen here, hairball. Kenny the Koala Bear's very life may be on the line here and you are toying with me. Do you know where Hannah is babysitting tonight or not?"

Puss Puss B' Guss Guss paused in his cleansing and now stood up in full form focused on the angry Bubba. "You know, Bubba, I was just thinking today--all the times we have been involved in cases together--all the times I have given you tidbits of information that have led to important discoveries--and do I even get a thank you? A special treat, like say, a box of fresh shrimp thrown my way? Oh, no--doesn't happen. But you! You get all the credit. The medals, the honors, the praise of your regiment, special T-bone steaks. Well, the Puss Puss has grown weary, Bubba. I need something special sometimes, too. This time, my information is <u>not</u> free. I want to be recognized as part and parcel of the hero perks package as well."

As angry as Bubba Doo Wah Wah was at the feline's coy ways at the moment, he had to admit, there was an element of truth in Puss Puss B' Guss Guss' statements. "All right, all right. If your information is solid and it leads to the rescue of Kenny, I promise that you will receive recognition by the Corps as well as a medal."

"I don't need a medal. Food and a photo op will do nicely. And make that fresh shrimp, <u>not</u> frozen."

"Done and done, my vain friend. Now, where is Hannah?"

With a dramatically uplifted tail, Puss Puss B' Guss Guss turned to re-enter the wine barrel, pausing, head turned back over his shoulder to look at Bubba Doo Wah Wah. "The Pomposity house... in the Land of Mean."

Chapter Twenty-Six

Pugnacious Pomposity, III's ears were beginning to ache. Greedy Gertie screaming out her stream of threats had been continual since the abrupt exodus from the banquet following the news from the home front. The elation from the early evening's affairs that Pugnacious had experienced now deflated like an aged, sun-worn balloon stuck in a tree.

"Gertie, really...calm yourself! You always make such a mountain out of a mole hill...and the spectacle that you caused tonight...it was downright humiliating."

"Humiliating?!" Mountain out of a mole hill?!! Oh, you will see a mountain tonight--a volcano explosion to be sure! The ones to be humiliated will be that no account Hannah. As for our sneak of a daughter, well, I'll tell you what will happen..." And Greedy Gertie was off and running again, at full volume no less. Pugnacious' head began to throb and his grip grew tighter on the wheel with an accompanying heavier lead foot on the accelerator pedal.

The realm of darkness' plan to have the whole forest burn down as well as Crystal Creek and outlying communities had been foiled due to the power of prayer. This unforeseen turn of events had

172

sent the emissaries of darkness, Grimely, Prurient, Odiferous and Hedgethorn, reeling. Looking to redeem themselves and not incur the scourges of Nocturnicon, they had taken off on this night's flight to see what other wickedness they could be part and parcel of. The unmistakable rage emanating from the stylish coupe below was instantly picked up on their radar.

"That is one of ours," hissed Prurient as the three hovered lower over the car following its rapid pace through the side streets.

"They both are," agreed Prurient.

"Let's get that anger stirred up to even greater heights and see what mischief could be ours tonight," intoned Grimely.

"Whoa, pull back a bit." For up ahead as the Pomposity car came to an abrupt halt in the driveway, the demons of darkness could see the Angels of Light, swords lifted upwards, positions stalwart. "We're at that blasted bear's house, the one we got chased out from!"

"Well, I say it's time for a return surprise attack. Make haste!"

Swooping unseen by the humans they followed behind, they made their swift entrance into the Pomposity home as Greedy Gertie and Pugnacious Pomposity, III entered through the front door. What the blackened creatures missed was that the angelic realm had left their roof top post and were now in the attic, poised and ready for battle.

With the return of Bubba Doo Wah Wah bearing the good news of Hannah and Kenny the Koala Bear's location, relief swept through the ranks. As the Ranger's truck barreled down the road to this long-awaited destination of Kenny's deliverance, the joy quickly dissipated into high alert status. The presence of evil was evident to all. The Ranger particularly sensed it in every fiber of his being as they approached the Pomposity residence. The Ranger had again parked the truck a few doors down from their destination, but, as they were now in the Land of Mean, no beautiful trees grew to hide their presence.

"What's the plan, Sr. Ranger?" Bubba queried as they neared the residence on foot and paws, spying the vehicle that had just arrived only seconds before them. The Ranger had been silently praying for wisdom and direction as they neared their quest's end. Just as the presence of evil grew stronger as they neared the house, so, to the Ranger's delight, did the presence of Light. "We're not alone men--there's a definite battle up ahead, but we're definitely <u>not</u> alone." He felt courage rise up within and the King's leading on the next step to take. "This way, gentlemen." The four hurriedly scurried across the rough rock front yard to the side of the house. The house was made of rough-hewn red brick. On the side that the Ranger directed them to was a white trellis that went almost up to the eaves beneath the house's roof. Interwoven throughout its squares was a gnarled, twisted, thick ashen wood vine that with imagination resembled a fairy tale stalk gone sorely wrong.

As the Ranger and the three Special Forces canines gazed upward at the surreal twisted form, the Ranger spoke. "He's up there, my men. I don't know how I know, but, Kenny is up there behind that window."

Chapter Twenty-Seven

The meeting tonight between Sallie the Singer of Songs, Hannah, and Kenny the Koala Bear had an overtone of foreboding. After the initial delight that Sallie always had when she unlocked her treasured trunk containing the precious cargo that had become friend, spiritual mentor, bear extraordinaire, she readily noticed that he was subdued, quiet, and even pensive.

"What's the matter, Kenny? You seem a bit sad." The Koala lovingly looked at the miracle of the King's transforming power that stood questioningly before him.

"Sit down little one, and Hannah. I do have something of great import to share with you tonight." Hannah and Sallie settled into the large, foam-filled cushions next to the antique trunk, faces expectant as well as apprehensive. "Do you remember," the Bear began, "at our first meeting together, Sallie, when I told you that I was on a mission and you asked me what a mission was?" Sallie nodded. "Well, at that time, I did not explain to you what that mission was because while I understood its meaning, I didn't fully understand the type of mission that I was on--what the purpose was, in other words." Kenny paused, looking at the faces so fixed upon him and attentiveness to each and every word he was to impart. "Well," he softly said, "now, I do."

"What is it, Kenny?" What do you mean?" Sallie interjected.

"My dear one, first of all, this is what a mission is. A mission is God's special direction for our lives. Once we come into the

Kingdom of Light when we receive the King of Kings and ask Him to be Lord of our lives, He changes us inside. And then, the inside flows out, like rivers of living water into the outside of our life. Your new name, Sallie the Singer of Songs, is a reflection of what His special direction, His special mission will be for your life. The songs He will give you that you will sing will change people's lives from wanting to follow the ways of darkness to wanting to follow the ways of Light."

Sallie smiled and felt joy as the wise koala's words filled her heart.

"My mission from the King of Kings was to be a witness of His Light in this Land of Mean where, until you said yes to Him and changed from Salena the Shrieker to Sallie the Singer of Songs, the Land of Mean had been under the total control of the Kingdom of Darkness."

At this, the Koala sat down, very close to both Sallie and Hannah. Taking Sallie's hands in his soft paws, he gazed intently at the eyes so full of life and light and said, "But now, my mission here is done, dear one, and I must return to my home in Crystal Creek--back to my family and to wait and listen for whatever the next adventure is to be. And, I must do so tonight."

"Tonight?! No, Kenny, no--it's just too soon! I don't want you to go. Who will I talk to? Who will teach me more about the King of Kings?" Big tears began to form in young Sallie's eyes and began to cascade down her cheeks. The Koala patted her hands and Hannah drew closer and put her arm around Sallie's shoulders. "Your King knows you have need of a friend and mentor--and He has so graciously provided one."

"Who, Kenny?" sobbed Sallie.

"She is sitting right next to you. She has been following the King for all of her young life and her parents have been following Him for a much, much longer time. They will be able to help you to grow in His ways, to follow His paths, to encourage you and be there for you to keep you from becoming discouraged. And, Miss Hannah here knows how to play the piano and I just believe that with her gift of music and your gift of song writing that some mighty praises could be written that would bring Glory to the King of Kings and Lord of Lords."

Hannah gave Sallie's shoulder a little squeeze. "I would love to do that with you, Sallie!"

Sallie wiped her eyes and managed a feeble smile at the thought of having a friend who she could talk to, but, the pain in her heart over the thought of Kenny the Koala Bear leaving still caused an ache inside. "But, Kenny--I have to live with my family and even when I sing my songs, it doesn't seem to make a difference."

"Patience, little one, patience. Give it time. Sometimes when people have been living in darkness, they don't like it when the light begins to shine upon them. Like I said before, you just be faithful to sing the songs. *"Let your light so shine before men, that they may see your good works, and glorify your Father which is in heaven." (Mat. 5:16).* Trust Him to do the rest. That is your mission, Sallie the Singer of Songs. To sing His songs and let His Light break forth as the dawn in this formerly, completely black Land of Mean."

"Will I ever see you again?"

"I don't know, little one--if it is His Will, it will be so. But, one thing I <u>do</u> know that you can count on is this:

"*For I am persuaded, that neither death, nor life, nor angels, nor principalities, nor powers, nor things present, nor things to come, nor height, nor depth nor any other creature, shall be able to separate us from the love of God, which is in...(Rom. 8:38-39)*

The tender, wise bear's words were abruptly drowned out by the most blood-curdling scream imaginable. Hannah and Sallie whirled about. Two unmistakable figures were clearly outlined in the attic's entryway: Greedy Gertie and Pugnacious Pomposity, III. In carpeted silence, they had crept up the attic stairs. Per Greedy Gertie's instructions, Horatio the Horrible had turned off all the inside house lights enabling him to lower the attic stairs without the betrayal of detection from light streaming in from below. He had then positioned himself in waiting at the front door, ever so quietly opening it when the Pomposities returned and parked in the front driveway thus avoiding the noise of the garage door opening and closing.

Now, Greedy Gertie's unintelligible, terrifying scream of rage formed into fear inducing words at the same volume and shrill pitch. "You little brats! How dare you come up in this attic, get into my trunk and take my bear. Give him to me this instant!"

Kenny the Koala Bear, as soon as the presence of the intruders was evident, had gone limp, falling forward into Sallie's lap. She now held him close to her, as she rose to her feet, wrapping her arms tighter around him, as Greedy Gertie drew closer. Hannah stood trembling beside her, equally terrified at Gertie's menacing advances. *What can we do--help us, my King--help us!*

Gertie was now directly in front of poor Sallie whose face was burrowed into Kenny's soft fur, refusing to look at the fearsome presence that was her mother. She too, silently, fervently, cried out in prayer to her King. *Help me--don't let her hurt Kenny!*

"Give him to me Salena--right now!" Greedy Gertie grabbed hold of Kenny the Koala Bear with her bony fingers digging deep into his soft fur, struggling to free him from Sallie's tight grip.

"No, momma, no--stop it--you're going to hurt him!"

"Let him loose, you little brat--he's mine!" And with one final yank, the Bear was in Greedy Gertie's clutches.

Ignoring the heartbroken, tearful cries and pleas of Sallie, Greedy Gertie held the Bear high over her head in triumph, securely out of the reach of Sallie who was jumping up and down trying to get him back.

"He's mine--all mine--all mine--and I'm going to put him where you will never find him again--ever!"

"No, momma, please, no!"

"Let me see, let me see!" Horatio the Horrible now burst upon the upper realm's mayhem. While scurrying behind Greedy Gertie and Pugnacious Pomposity, III's ascent into the attic, he had tripped and slid backwards down the stairs due to his stocking feet. Now, barreling full steam ahead toward momma Gertie to get a better view of the Bear on high, he couldn't stop in time and crashed into Gertie's side with such force that she fell sideways into a large collection of precariously balanced cardboard boxes piled almost to the ceiling. In a panic to grasp for something to brace herself as she lost her balance, she released her grip on the Bear and Kenny went airborne, landing on the wide ledge in front of the dusty attic window.

In the unseen realm of the attic, a brief, but fierce battle had raged. The emissaries of darkness' hopes for an evil outcome was short lived. The four angels of Light, swords held high, were well prepared for this final ambush. Their presence remained concealed until the demons cackled their victory cry as Greedy Gertie held Kenny the Koala Bear high above her head. At that very moment, the Angels of Light swooped down upon the enemy forces, and with a blinding flash of swords, the underworld forces quickly lost their hold upon the human world.

At the sight of Greedy Gertie falling, Pugnacious Pomposity, III rushed to try and stop the inevitable, but it was too late. The three Pomposities lay temporarily out of commission from further pursuit of the Bear as they struggled to free themselves from the boxes, loose clothing and bedding that now entangled them in a grand, dirt filled heap.

"Quickly, Hannah, Sallie--help me to open this window."

Hannah and Sallie, before so horrified at the evil that had been taking place, now gleefully sprang into action to help the Koala.

179

They clambered up to where Kenny was now struggling to free the latch on the dirt-encased window. Sallie's little fingers just weren't strong enough. "Hannah, you try." Hannah pulled and pulled with her good arm, but it just wouldn't budge.

"Hurry, Hannah, hurry" urged Sallie.

"I'm trying...I'm trying..."

As Hannah struggled with the stuck latch with Kenny and Sallie intently cheering her on, she prayed, *Lord, we're so close--Kenny has to go home, please my King, give me strength.*

An unseen and unfelt hand from one of the commissioned angels from on high placed his hand over Hannah's. The other three angels had already exited this musty space in hot pursuit of the arrogant emissaries of darkness whose battle with the mighty forces of the King had ended in stinging defeat.

The window suddenly broke free of the old bent latch, and cool night air rushed in as the window swung open. Sallie gave the Koala Bear one last hug. "I'm going to miss you so much, Kenny."

The Bear replied, "I will miss you too, little one. But remember, dear Sallie, your songs will inspire the hearts of others to love and serve the King of Kings. You must go forth on your mission now, Sallie the Singer of Songs." Looking back at both Hannah and Sallie as he grasped the trellis and gnarled vine, he swung his body over the ledge, and said, "We will be together in Spirit." Kenny the Koala Bear then began his precarious descent down the trellis wall, claws extending, grasping each thick branch as he inched downward.

At the swinging open of the window, the team below took cover behind an outdoor shed in the corner. The Ranger silently motioned the canines to be alert and ready and that he would hold back in the shadows until Kenny was on the ground. Realizing that if Hannah saw him, the mission could be compromised, he pulled the parka hood of his jacket up over his head in anticipation of the upcoming flight his forces would make once Kenny was securely in tow.

As Hannah and Sallie watched the Koala's careful descent to freedom, the muffled sounds of the three Pomposities buried beneath the mound of boxes could be heard as they were loosing themselves bit by bit from the tangled mess.

"Oh, Hannah--what if they get free before he gets away? They'll lock him up for good!"

An idea popped into Hannah's mind almost the instant Sallie had posed her question. *Must be the Lord's inspiration.* "Don't worry, Sallie. He only needs a few more moments. You stay here."

With great haste, Hannah climbed down from the window ledge and fled past the struggling Pomposities, back down the carpeted attic stairs. Standing on the chair still in place, she punched the button that raised the stairs back up into the ceiling and kept her finger on it, knowing that if they tried to open it up top, it would not work. (A little bit of mechanical knowledge she had learned from helping her dad on some of his home repair projects).

Sallie, meanwhile, continued to watch the descent of her beloved Kenny as the sounds of her family were growing louder in the background. As she gazed at the departure of her friend with mixed emotion racing through her heart, she was suddenly privileged to see the most amazing scene unfold before her young eyes. Three dogs and a man emerged from the shadows below and positioned themselves beneath the trellis, as though expecting the escape of the Koala to occur. She saw Kenny the Koala Bear suddenly catch glimpse of the large golden retriever and heard his shout of glee: "My old friend!" together with the resounding friendly barks back in return. *The King must have arranged this strange rescue team--He must have known--Kenny told me He knows everything! And, He gave me that new special name...*

And then it hit her--just as the Koala let loose of the old gnarled vine and landed upon the retriever's back, saddle style, Sallie the Singer of Songs leaned out the window and hollered with all her might:

"Kenny! You never told me my King's name. What's His name, Kenny? What's His name?"

As Kenny the Koala Bear, the three Special Canine Forces and Rick the Red-Necked Ranger went forth in high gear run, Kenny proclaimed the Name that is above every name, the Name that who-soever shall call upon that Name, shall live in the Kingdom of Light forever and be saved from the Kingdom of Darkness.

"His Name?" shouted Kenny for all the world to hear as he took off on the back of Bubba Doo Wah Wah into the night, "His Name... is......JESUS!!!"

CPSIA information can be obtained
at www.ICGtesting.com
Printed in the USA
FFOW02n1031110615
14179FF